ASES IN ORGANIZATIONAL COMMUNICATION

Cases in Organizational Communication

A Lifespan Approach

Ryan S. Bisel
University of Oklahoma

Michael W. Kramer
University of Oklahoma

New York   Oxford
OXFORD UNIVERSITY PRESS

Oxford University Press is a department of the University of Oxford.
It furthers the University's objective of excellence in research, scholarship,
and education by publishing worldwide. Oxford is a registered trademark of
Oxford University Press in the UK and certain other countries.

Published in the United States of America by Oxford University Press
198 Madison Avenue, New York, NY 10016, United States of America.

© 2020 by Oxford University Press

Library of Congress Cataloging-in-Publication Data
Names: Bisel, Ryan S., author. | Kramer, Michael W., author.
Title: Cases in organizational communication / Ryan S. Bisel, University of
    Oklahoma, Michael W. Kramer, University of Oklahoma.
Description: New York, NY : Oxford University Press, [2020]
Identifiers: LCCN 2019010850 (print) | LCCN 2019013522 (ebook) |
    ISBN 9780190925451 (ebook) | ISBN 9780190925444 (pbk.)
Subjects: LCSH: Communication in organizations—Case studies.
Classification: LCC HD30.3 (ebook) | LCC HD30.3 .B57 2020 (print) |
    DDC 658.4/5—dc23
LC record available at https://lccn.loc.gov/2019010850

Printing number: 9 8 7 6 5 4 3 2 1
Printed by Sheridan Books, Inc., United States of America

CONTENTS

PREFACE

This collection of case studies is the first of its kind to be constructed as a companion to an organizational communication textbook—namely, *Organizational Communication: A Lifespan Approach* (Kramer & Bisel, 2017). Years of interacting with students has shown us the value of presenting true-to-life stories of organizational experiences alongside organizational concepts and theories. Stories have that special power to engage the mind, memory, and emotions. Our hope is that these stories will be helpful in engaging students' exploration of organizational communication—a topic that can seem abstract at first glance. Yet this collection provides instructors and students with a wealth of opportunities to see, hear, and feel how the fleeting nature of words can and does shape organizations and our experiences in them.

Gathering and editing this collection is a labor of love for us. Of course, we love the topic of organizational communication, but we also love hearing, collecting, and telling stories that illustrate the power and relevance of this topic. Listen and you will hear that stories about organizational communication are all around us. Perhaps there's even something about communicating in organizations that motivates people to enjoy sharing stories about them. Such stories are common in everyday gossip, humorous anecdotes, venting sessions, blame placing, praising, prayer requests, informal envisioning, frustrated dreaming, advice giving, biographies, and autobiographies. These organizational communication stories are a window into the human experience: They are filled with heroes and villains, courage and cowardice, highs and lows.

While this collection could be used as a stand-alone text, creating it alongside our existing textbook means that we were able to integrate the following unique features:

- First, in the Appendix, we provide a **Quick-Reference Table** that indicates which textbook chapters are most obviously illustrated by each case (see page **165**).
- Second, and relatedly, each case concludes with thought-provoking **Discussion Questions** that correspond to the content presented in two or three main chapters in the textbook.

- Third, in keeping with the focus on **ethics** throughout the textbook, the majority of cases include **Discussion Questions** designed to foster deeper reflection on the ethical implications of characters' communication.
- Fourth, the beginning of each case indicates its origin or inspiration with a **footnote**. Some cases are based in personal experience or firsthand consulting with organizations. Meanwhile, still other cases are based on published empirical data collected in the field or experiment setting. Instructors may wish to pair these cases with the published article(s) that inspired it.
- Fifth, cases include a **Suggested Readings** section that identifies related empirical and peer-review works, which instructors could pair with the reading for more advanced students.

We hope you enjoy this collection and exploring more about organizational communication.

Sincerely,
Ryan and Michael

ACKNOWLEDGMENTS

Our sincere thanks are extended to reviewers of this text. They include the following:

Abby Brooks, Georgia Southern University
Jacqueline Bruscella, State University of New York, College at Oneonta
Veronica Dawson, California State University Stanislaus
John Meyer, University of Southern Mississippi

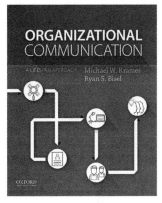

The Lifespan Approach In

Organizational Communication
Michael W. Kramer, *University of Oklahoma*
Ryan S. Bisel, *University of Oklahoma*

How it Works: The lifespan approach helps students understand their organizational experiences across their lifetime. Kramer and Bisel begin their book by showing how our pre-career experiences influence our organizational experiences (Chapter 2: Anticipatory Socialization, Chapter 3: Organizational Encounter) and end with organizational transitions and exit, including retirement.

Advantages: This approach situates students in context and shows how theories and perspectives apply across time. Beginning with socialization provides students with exposure to the field on a subject we can all relate to and helps ground the study of organizational communication not only in large for-profit companies but all types of organizations, including volunteer organizations—a unique area of coverage in Kramer & Bisel.

What it's not: This approach is a way of organizing the current body of knowledge of organizational communication in a way that is contextual and student-friendly, but it's not a rigid system that needs to dictate or change how you teach. Chapters can be moved around or omitted as you might do with any textbook you assign.

What faculty are saying: *Sarah Riforgiate, Kansas State University:* "I commend this approach because it shows how the same theories apply across time and contexts as students experience different life events. I also appreciate the applied nature – students can walk away with theory that they can use directly to enhance their organizational experiences."

5 Reasons to Choose:

Organizational Communication
Michael W. Kramer, *University of Oklahoma*
Ryan S. Bisel, *University of Oklahoma*

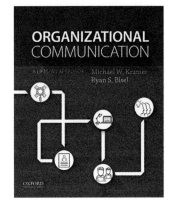

1. **The only organizational communication textbook written with beginning students in mind.**
   Full of real-world stories, helpful and unique illustrations, and constant application of theory and perspectives, Kramer and Bisel have provided a truly student-focused introduction to the field.

2. **The lifespan approach helps students understand their organizational experiences across their lifetime.**
   Kramer and Bisel begin by showing how our pre-career experiences influence our organizational experiences and end with organizational exit, including retirement. This approach situates students in context and shows how theories apply across time.

3. **Each chapter begins with a relatable, real-world scenario.**
   Kramer and Bisel draw students in with relatable stories and use these stories throughout the chapter to apply concepts and perspectives. Application features throughout incorporate important lessons for students.

4. **Ethical issues are integrated into every chapter.**
   Kramer and Bisel discuss ethics throughout, including ethical issues features in each chapter that place students in a real-world scenario and prompt them to think about ethical decision-making.

5. **Unique chapters on anticipatory socialization, assimilation, power, and work-life balance.**
   From the theoretical to the practical, Kramer and Bisel have focused on not only the cutting edge research in the discipline, but seamlessly integrate it through topics students care about.

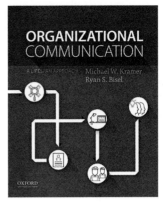

Applied, Relatable, Engaging

Organizational Communication
Michael W. Kramer, *University of Oklahoma*
Ryan S. Bisel, *University of Oklahoma*

Jaesub Lee, University of Houston: "It is very conversational, relatable, and easy to follow with everyday examples. It reads extremely well and flows smoothly with a terrific integration of diverse sets of ideas. My students will love it."

Frances Smith, Murray State University: "This book provides a straightforward, clear description of important processes involved in organizational communication as they relate to students' daily lives. The examples and scenarios are relatable and engaging. Research and theories are provided consistently throughout to enlighten the students on the important elements of each concept."

Sarah Riforgiate, Kansas State University: "I commend this approach because it shows how the same theories apply across time and contexts as students experience different life events. I also appreciate the applied nature – students can walk away with theory that they can use directly to enhance their organizational experiences."

Kathy Krone, University of Nebraska: "Positioning case material in the form of a scenario at the beginning of each chapter is a creative approach to help engage students with the conceptual material early in the reading process."

Stephanie Dailey, Texas State University: "I really like the scenarios at the start of each chapter. The story is broad enough so that a wide range of students can imagine themselves in the scenario, but the narrative still includes enough detail so that students can see the concepts at play. The application section does a wonderful job of explicitly tying the scenario to concepts discussed throughout the chapter."

Jeremy Fyke: Belmont University: "The scenarios and overall lifespan approach are distinguishing features that help to place students in the real context. Related to that, the communication challenges and ethical issues are great features that help reinforce the applied approach to the book."

Angela Gist, University of Kansas: "This text is a must have for your organizational communication class. Not only is the content extremely well-written and comprehensive it is also personable, relevant, and accessible."

Organizational Communication
Michael Kramer, University of Oklahoma
Ryan Bisel, University of Oklahoma

466 pages
eBook: $34.95
9780190606312

Loose-leaf: $48.99
9780190649340

Paperback: $69.95
9780190606268

STRATEGIC AMBIGUITY, IDEOLOGY, AND HEGEMONIC PARTICIPATION IN THE YELP ELITE SQUAD

David A. Askay, PhD
California Polytechnic State University

Emelyn moved from California to the East Coast to pursue a graduate degree. Arriving in the city of Chester, she began using Yelp to acquaint herself with the restaurants and businesses in the area. She also started writing reviews of her own experiences, just for fun.

After a few months and two dozen reviews, Emelyn received an email inviting her to join the Yelp Elite Squad for 2012. This was unexpected, because she had never heard of the Elite Squad nor did she know what they did. Clicking on a link in the email brought her to a webpage with a description:

> You've heard legends about their reviews, their shiny profile badges, and—of course—their epic parties. But the Yelp Elite Squad is even more than that. Members of this exclusive, in-the-know crew reveal hot spots for fellow locals, act as city ambassadors, and are the true heart of the Yelp community, both on and offline.

This chapter is based on personal experiences and published work: Askay, D. A., & Gossett, L. (2015). Concealing communities within the crowd: Hiding organizational identities and brokering member identifications of the Yelp Elite Squad. *Management Communication Quarterly*, *29*(4), 616–641.

The website added that "the Elite Council spends many a sleepless night with pizza, beer, and 5-Hour Energy shots to pore over individual profiles and figure out who deserves another coveted term in office."

Emelyn learned that each year the Elite Council selected who joined or retained membership in the Elite Squad. Those selected were invited to exclusive free events each month, which were coordinated by a local community manager. Although joining required her to add her real name and photo on her profile, Emelyn was enticed by the possibilities. After complying with these terms, a red badge appeared on her Yelp profile that said *Elite '12.*

In retrospect, she had seen this badge on some reviewers in the past but never thought much about it. Now she was excited to discover that it meant so much.

She soon received an email invitation to an upcoming Elite Event from Bethany, the local community manager for Chester. The event required that she RSVP by clicking on her Elite badge to access a private section of the Yelp website. Doing so revealed a calendar of upcoming events, photos from previous events, and some behavioral guidelines for Elites (such as *Don't use your badge to demand special treatment*). Emelyn also saw that she could bring a guest. She decided to invite Will, her friend from school.

Two days before the event, she received an email exclaiming "*You're In!*" and providing her with details about the location and time of the event.

After arriving, Bethany quickly recognized and welcomed Emelyn. Looking around, Emelyn was impressed at having a private room in the restaurant for the 30+ attendees. The mood was playful and fun: People were in costumes and taking silly photos. Bethany directed her to a table filled with Yelp-branded pins, mints, and lip balm, where Emelyn and Will helped themselves to the swag.

Walking around, they were offered free wine, beer, and hors d'oeuvres carried by well-dressed servers. This culminated in an upscale three-course meal.

As the meal arrived, Bethany announced, "Thank you all for coming and being such an integral part of the Chester Elite Squad. This community wouldn't exist without all that you do. Yelp really appreciates your hard work! Now, please welcome the head chef to introduce the amazing meal that she put together for you!"

At their table, Emelyn and Will spoke with Joshi and Amber, two longtime Elite members. Being new and unsure what it meant to be Elite, Emelyn asked, "So, how does one even become Elite? I have no idea how I was selected."

Joshi, an Elite member with over 2,000 reviews, answered, "That is a very good question! I have no idea. Supposedly there is a committee in San Francisco that evaluates your reviews and goes 'Yes, this person is worthy' and 'No, this person is not.' I have heard all sorts of things. I have no idea of any actual facts."

"So, what do you think it takes?" replied Emelyn, "Like writing a certain number of reviews?"

Amber responded, "Yeah, the number of reviews probably plays a role. I challenge myself to write one review each day, but I think being Elite really means that you are *Yelpy* and represent the community well. You've taken the time to give thoughtful, objective reviews and not let your emotions come into play. Just because I might be really upset with an experience doesn't mean that I am going to write an entirely bad review. I might say, 'This was bad, but this was also pretty good in this area.' Look at Joshi's review of Cafe Luna! Most people just throw a five-star at it, but I like his nuanced description about how it was noisy and had unfriendly servers. Now I know not to bring my parents there when they visit."

Joshi added, "I think that sometimes five is like the 'unattainable five-star rating.' It is really hard to want to give five stars because it would have to exceed my expectations. And I don't want to just repeat what everyone else says. I want to add that extra insight: the ambiance, the sound, the parking."

Hearing this made sense to Emelyn. Being Elite suggested that she should have more discriminating tastes and higher expectations. Finishing her meal, she was inspired to take her reviewing really seriously.

As the event concluded, Bethany thanked everyone once again. She encouraged the guests of the Elites to write reviews so that they, too, could join the Elite community.

Going home afterward, Emelyn and Will were giddy with excitement. Being graduate students on a budget, they were not accustomed to such fine dining—let alone getting it for free. Will made Emelyn promise to invite him again as her +1 for the next event.

Over the next few days, Emelyn was preoccupied with Yelp. She visited her profile frequently to see how many people liked her reviews, accepted friend requests, and read messages from people from the event. She also kept tabs on the number of *Useful*, *Funny*, and *Cool* votes that she garnered for her reviews. All this motivated Emelyn to write more. Inspired by Amber, she wanted to write one review each day. She became strategic, listing out all her favorite local businesses that she would review.

Starting on the first restaurant, she described the excellent food and décor. It seemed like an easy five-star restaurant. However, she paused, remembering her conversation with Joshi. Emelyn pondered, *"Was it really a five-star experience?"* Expanding her review, she described other aspects of her experience—the dreadful parking and slow-to-arrive appetizers. She then assigned a four-star rating and felt proud of her decision.

The next day, the review had already garnered seven *Useful* votes. Emelyn was elated.

Over the next week, Emelyn wrote 10 more reviews for her favorite places. Although each one took her about 45 minutes to write, the accompanying compliments and votes from other users made it feel worthwhile.

Two weeks later, she received another email from Bethany announcing the upcoming Elite Event. She noted that space was limited, so only active Elites would be able to attend.

Emelyn again RSVP'd with Will as her guest, but this time she felt insecure. She thought, *"Have I been active enough in the community? What can I do in the next week?"* She reached out to Amber for advice.

"What I do," answered Amber, "is make sure that I post in the online forums. Like, answering a question or responding to something that Bethany posted. I also vote on reviews and send compliments to people. Sometimes I go out of my way to visit a new place to review."

Emelyn resolved to follow this advice. During the next week, Emelyn devoted some of her evenings to participating in the online forums and sending messages to other reviewers. She also made a list of new restaurants that she planned to visit.

That Friday when she went out to dinner with friends, she encouraged them to drive a bit farther to try Injera, a place on her list.

Their visit did not start well: The parking lot was filled and the wait to get seated took 30 minutes. Things did not improve after they sat down. It took nearly 20 minutes for their order to be taken, and the waiter never once refilled their water. Finally, the food was okay, but it took almost 45 minutes to come out, and when it did, it was cold.

Throughout dinner Emelyn was verbally critiquing the experience to her friends. At first, they agreed. However, they grew annoyed at her commentary.

"Please stop fixating on everything and just try to make the best of it," Vladimir stated.

As the conversation turned toward *Game of Throne* theories, Emelyn became aloof as she remained attentive to the details of her experience and used her phone to draft out her review.

At her computer that night, Emelyn concluded that this dinner was among her worst experiences. However, she remained balanced in crafting her review and described her experience fully, even complimenting the delicious injera.

Then she paused to think about the one-star rating she wanted to assign. Thinking of the number of votes and compliments she received for reviews, Emelyn grew concerned that as an Elite member her negative review had the potential to harm the business. She was also acutely aware that her real name and photo were attached to this review. She thought, *"What would my friends think if they saw the review? What if the owner recognized me somewhere?"* Wrestling with these thoughts, Emelyn ultimately decided to bump up her rating to two stars.

The next day, she received a compliment from Bethany stating, "You're well on your way to 30 reviews! That makes me want to talk in L33T speak . . . 0h y34h! S0 s1ck!"[1] Accompanying this was an email saying, "You're In!" for the next Elite event.

---

1 "L33T speak" is an online vernacular that swaps Latin characters with visually similar ASCII characters. Here, *L33T* is short for the word *elite*.

The proceeding months were an exciting and busy time. Emelyn wrote over 60 reviews, frequently attended events, and befriended many Elites. More and more, she felt connected to the Elite Squad community.

Will had even been selected to join the Elite Squad after he began writing reviews and Emelyn nominated him. Now they each brought new friends to the Elite events.

Then one day, Emelyn invited her friend Loralei to attend an event.

Confused, Loralei inquired about the Elite Squad. She was surprised to learn about the amount of time and money Emelyn devoted to visiting and reviewing new, out-of-the-way businesses. Loralei said, "Yelp is a multimillion-dollar corporation that is making tons of money off your reviews. Why do you devote so much to them when it sounds like you are just working for free? What is your role in Yelp's business?"

Emelyn was taken aback. She never considered her participation from this perspective. She responded, "I've always seen the Elite Squad as a community. I never really thought of it as being part of a business. I just felt like, 'Oh, it's just a fun community' and that my friends are in it. Of course, I enjoyed the free food and drinks, but I also enjoyed helping people in Chester. I've never thought of myself as like a volunteer or a worker. Not even a part of Yelp. Just, I guess, I thought of myself as a community member. But the community manager is a paid employee of Yelp, so maybe I am like a volunteer or something."

The conversation moved on, but Emelyn continued to ruminate on it. *"Was I somehow duped into working for free and making money for Yelp?"* she thought.

During the following weeks, Emelyn felt increasingly disillusioned with the Elite Squad. On top of that, her schooling became more intense. Her motivation and time to review dwindled. Emphasizing this, she was not admitted to the next Elite Event.

Every few weeks, Bethany sent her a message like "Been a while since your last review. Where have you been lately? I'd love to read some new ones soon!"

After 3 months, Emelyn received a final email:

To: Emelyn

From: Bethany

I just wanted to check in. I got a note from the Elite Council that said you were at risk for losing your Elite badge since you weren't writing reviews anymore. There are only so many spots that can go to Elites and they look at it a few times a year to make sure they shouldn't shift them around to other Yelpers. Remember, being Elite means that you are a model Yelper for the rest of the community in adding the most useful, funny, and cool reviews, photos, and tips. You're a great writer and we need you! I hope everything's okay your way. Come back to us if you can!

DISCUSSION QUESTIONS

1. Organizations can be defined legally, communicatively, and socially. Using this framework, in what ways can the Elite Squad be considered an organization? What are the organizational boundaries, if any, between the Elite Squad and Yelp Inc.?

2. Some members of the Elite Squad were unclear on what precisely it took to be selected. Evaluate this as an example of *strategic ambiguity*. Discuss the value of providing Elite Squad members with ambiguous performance expectations for the organization.

3. How might more precise requirements for membership in the Elite Squad alter the behavior and expectations of reviewers? Is this an ethical or unethical use of strategic ambiguity?

4. How is surface power exercised in relationship to members of the Elite Squad? Identify the resource dependencies and social exchanges that operate in this context.

5. While Emelyn thought of her participation in the Elite Squad as *being a community member*, Loralei suggested that Emelyn was an *unpaid worker*. Consider these labels as they relate to deep structure power and ideology. How might some Elite Squad members be oppressed by the way they understand their participation?

6. The critical approach to organizational communication often seeks to emancipate people from oppressive ideologies. Discuss this in relation to Loralei's comments using the concepts of *sensebreaking* and *sensegiving*. Explain the ethical issues that one should consider when given the opportunity to emancipate an organizational member from an ideology.

SUGGESTED READINGS

Askay, D. A., & Gossett, L. (2015). Concealing communities within the crowd: Hiding organizational identities and brokering member identifications of the Yelp Elite Squad. *Management Communication Quarterly, 29*, 616–641.

Barmann, J. (2014, August 13). Yelp Elite Reviewers suing company (again) for unpaid wages, claiming they are real writers. *SFist*. Retrieved from http://sfist.com/2014/08/13/yelp_elite_reviewers_suing_company.php

Scholz, T. (Ed.). (2012). *Digital labor: The Internet as playground and factory*. New York, NY: Routledge.

Scott, C. (2013). *Anonymous agencies, backstreet businesses, and covert collectives: Rethinking organizations in the 21st century*. Stanford, CA: Stanford University Press.

PUBLICLY AVAILABLE ARTIFACTS

Yelp Public Photo Gallery—https://www.flickr.com/photos/yelp/albums/
Yelp Elite FAQ—http://www.yelp.com/elite

SHIFTING WORKFORCE @ THE WORKPLACE

BEST PRACTICE CASE STUDY ON EMPLOYEE ENGAGEMENT AND ORGANIZATIONAL DIVERSITY

Kate M. Delmo, PhD
University of Technology Sydney

It was Lily's first day at work as a full-time employee of the Global Banking Corporation (GBC), one of the largest banks operating in Australia. Her Welcome Kit sent to her by the Human Resources (HR) Department indicated that newly hired employees were required to attend the Employee Orientation at the Sydney headquarters office.

"Hi, Lily!" Lily turned around and saw David Walters, GBC's Human Resource Manager, waving at her.

Lily met David at the second round of interviews when she was applying for her job as an account executive at the Loans Department. She was happy to see a familiar face that morning. The greeting calmed her nerves a bit.

"Hello, David. I am excited to be here," Lily said.

"We are glad that you can make it. I assume that your staff ID works?"

"It did. I used it to access the lifts this morning. Thank you for mailing it to me with the rest of GBC's Welcome Kit."

"My pleasure. Anyway, help yourself with some morning tea. Feel free to sit anywhere inside the Mangrove Function room. The program will start in about 15 minutes."

This chapter is based on in-class workshop activity on organizational diversity for the subject "54045 Organisational Communication" at the University of Technology Sydney, Australia.

"Sure. Thanks, David."

Lily went to the refreshments bar and got herself a cup of coffee. She looked around to take it all in. GBC was Lily's second major employer after graduating from the university. Lily recalled that in her previous workplace, she was very nervous on her first day at work. Her supervisor gave her a list of tasks that needed to be accomplished during the next financial quarter. Lily recalled feeling overwhelmed. There were no orientation programs either. However, her supervisor was kind to introduce her to a few colleagues near her work station. *"But I had to learn about things on my own since Day One,"* Lily thought to herself.

After finishing her coffee, Lily walked toward the function room. On her way there, she saw small booths lined up by the entrance. There were several persons idly chatting near the booths.

Upon seeing Lily, one of them approached her and greeted, "Hello, welcome to Employee Orientation Day! I'm Alice, an account executive here at Global Bank."

"Hi, Alice. I'm Lily."

"You must have read about GBC's Employee Action Groups in your Welcome Kit. I am a member of one of them. My colleagues and I set up these pop-up booths to give some information to GBC's new staff like you."

"Yes, the groups sound very interesting! I believe the CEO will talk about it as well later at the program?"

"He will indeed! We love this bank initiative for employees. Let me know if you have questions about the groups at some point. I would be happy to help."

"Got it, thanks."

"Okay, I think the program is about to start. I will see you inside, Lily."

"Will do, thank you."

Lily went inside the function room and sat in one of the middle-row seats. She immediately noticed that GBC has a culturally diverse workforce. She saw employees from at least three different ethnic backgrounds just with a quick glance at people who were seated next to her.

Lily mustered her courage and introduced herself to a few of them. "Hi, I'm Lily. How are you?"

"Hello, I'm Zihen Chu," said the girl from an Asian background.

"Are you also a new employee?" Lily asked.

"Yes, I am with Corporate Affairs. You?"

"I am with the Finance Group, Loans Department."

"Hi, I am Olima," said another employee with a distinct Polynesian accent. "Pleasure to meet you both."

"Which department are you with, Olima?" Zihen asked.

"I'm with HR. I take it we are all newbies today!" Olima remarked.

"Yes, we are. Are you both excited?" Lily asked.

"I am. I just graduated from college. This is my first job so I am not really sure what to do," Zihen replied.

"You will be okay. This is my third full-time job. My previous colleagues said that GBC takes care of its employees. So, let's see," Olima said smiling.

"That's right, we'll see," Lily said thoughtfully. "*I am beginning to love the vibe here,*" she said to herself.

The program started. The company's current Chief Executive Officer (CEO) and Managing Director (MD) Brian Harper delivered the Welcome Address. Lily was thrilled to know that she is now a part of an organization with 40,000 employees spread across branches in Australia, which offers a range of financial services to its clients.

What piqued Lily's interest the most was when Brian introduced GBC's Inclusion and Diversity initiative. Brian explained details of the program in his speech. "In this changing communication landscape, we recognize that an engaged, happy workforce is core to the success of a company. We also acknowledge that the bank is attracting employees from various cultural backgrounds. We think this is our key, competitive asset as a company—our diverse workforce. We define diversity as differences of thought or perspectives in the organization. To us, diversity breeds creativity. Creativity leads to innovation. We put a premium on innovation because this gives us an edge in our ever-competitive and complex business environment.

"Attracting creative, talented employees is one thing. Making them stay is another. So, we decided to identify what will make them do just that—stay with us. In 2010, Global Bank conducted an employee engagement survey that served as a basis for our strategy in encouraging a diverse and inclusive workplace. A key insight from the survey was inclusion. The report we submitted to the Diversity Council Australia entitled 'Taking Action' explains that inclusion is the extent to which employees feel included and valued. We learned that when employees have a strong sense of belonging at work: (a) better ideas are created, (b) employees feel valued, and (c) employees are inspired to initiate activities tailored to their needs.

"We were thrilled to learn from the survey that our employees have strong advocacies that they hold dear. Supporting our employees' advocacies means supporting other things important to them apart from work. This was our guiding principle when we developed our 'Champions for Inclusion' program that encouraged employees to form nine advocacy streams. We called the streams our 'Employee Action Groups' or EAGs."

Lily looked at the EAG brochure included in her Welcome Kit. She remembered the pop-up booths outside the program venue. "*This is so interesting,*" Lily muttered to herself as she had another quick read of information about the groups (see Table 2.1).

At that point, Brian invited questions from the audience. Joining him on a panel were Alice Thun Nguyen and Antonio Bartoli. Alice was the one whom Lily met at the EAG booths. Antonio was a senior executive in the bank who worked closely with EAGs.

Table 2.1. Employee Action Groups (EAGs) of Westpac Banking Corporation

EAG	Vision, Mission and Goals
ABLE: Assisting Better Lives for Everyone (Accessibility)	Advocates for customers and employees with disability or accessibility requirements
Anti-Family Violence (AFV)	Provides training, support, and tools to equip and empower individuals and families experiencing violence in the home to move toward a life free of violence, now and for future generations
Asian Leadership	Actively engages, mentors, and sponsors members to develop future leaders and improve Asian cultural awareness across GBC Group
Brothers & Sisters (Indigenous Australians)	Provides a network for Indigenous and non-Indigenous employees who share a common vision for a workplace where Indigenous Australians and culture are understood, respected, and celebrated
FLEX (Workplace flexibility)	Supports employees, leaders, and teams to think differently about how, when, and where work is conducted
GLOBAL (LGBTI)	Helps build a safe and respectful work environment for all LGBTI employees; one that values diversity, creating a culture of equality and inclusion
Prime of Life (employees over age 50)	Influences how GBC supports and develops mature employees, offering a range of information and contacts who can help with interests specific to this age group
WOW (Women of Westpac) (Women in leadership)	Empowers women of GBC to make confident career choices through education, information, and networking opportunities
Youth (employees under age 30)	Unites aspiring young people across GBC Group to help them reach their full potential and, in turn, develop as future leaders

Source: Diversity Council Australia Report (2015).

One member of the audience opened the session. "Thank you, Brian, for welcoming us. To Alice or Antonio, could you tell us about the EAG initiative from a member's perspective?"

Alice answered, "Sure. Employee Action Groups give us employees a chance to work together with like-minded colleagues to promote our respective advocacies to senior management. It is a platform for us to bring into discussion some of our concerns, issues, or challenges. Of course, this is in relation to our work. Members sort of act as volunteers who advocate for business needs important to their respective groups.

"Each EAG is given a small operating budget every year to support our initiatives. We think of different activities that are fun and engaging for our members. For example, I am a member of *FLEX*, the group that puts forward suggestions about flexible working arrangements for employees. As a mother of two very young children with no other support system here aside from my partner, it is challenging for me to be in the office from 9 a.m. to 5 p.m. every day, 5 days a week due to our kids' drop-off and pick-up schedules. FLEX is advocating for some staff to be allowed to work from home maybe once a week or 2 days per fortnight. This, of course, needs to be carefully planned with your team or department manager. But at least employees like me feel that senior management *knows*. It helps when we are able to tell management about this," Alice explained.

"Could you give us more examples of activities initiated by other EAGs?" asked another employee.

Alice replied, "A few will be creating opportunities for networking events. The Youth EAG is big on this. Other groups focus on creating platforms for continued education or training. Some EAGs identified ways to embed inclusion practices into the bank's daily operations. ABLE, for example, has consulted with GBC's Group Property Division about integrating intuitive accessibility designs into employee work stations in some of our Melbourne and Sydney offices. Without ABLE's initiative on this, senior management may not fully understand how to support employees with special needs."

Lily raised her hand. "Does a group directly report to the CEO of the company?"

"Yes," Brian answered. "At the start of every financial year, EAGs submit their strategic plans for the year to ensure that their proposed initiatives are in line with the bank's Inclusion and Diversity Policy. I read their plans and consult the Board about which ones to prioritize for that year.

"I have to say, though, that priority setting is challenging for us. In as much as we want to support all EAG activities, our resources are also limited. The Board decides which concern needs to be addressed first, and what resources to allocate.

"Alice's point on flexible working arrangements, for example, is continuously being discussed. Umm, we are proud that we have taken baby steps on this. Some employees are able to make a case to their team leaders about working from home. However, given our 40,000 strong employee base, we want to be careful on our policy about this. We want to make sure that alternative arrangements will not disrupt our daily operations. In short, employees and their teams should be able to hit their KPIs regardless if they work in the office or at home," Brian said.

"What about outcomes expected from EAGs?" asked another member of the audience.

Antonio answered the question. "Outcomes of all EAGs are presented directly to our Chief Executive Officer on a quarterly basis. It is a means to assure senior management that groups are achieving their objectives. Each EAG is assigned a senior executive who serves as the mentor of the group. This is my current role for the group called 'Brothers and Sisters.' My job is to make sure that members are able to articulate objectives of their proposed activities in their strategic plans. I also read their year-end report to check if it specifies whether targets are met. The bank would also like to know if they still remained efficient in their jobs while working on their EAG activities."

"We have to remember, though, that each EAG is only given a small amount of money for their activities," Brian exclaimed. "GBC is not expecting too much from what is given to them as long as employees use these groups as an avenue for collaboration. The bank wants them to have fun working on their advocacies! I think that is the main point."

Olami joined the discussion. "Alice, is membership in a group really fun?"

"Absolutely!" Alice replied. "Having a direct line of communication with the CEO is crucial to us. Having said this, however, I have to admit that building consensus among members does not come easy all the time. Just like in any other group, there are personality differences. Diverse ideas abound. But on days when we get all excited about what we want to tell senior management, we go back to the vision of the group. EAGs were created to encourage employee engagement. So discussions, deliberations, and negotiations on what should be prioritized by the group are welcomed. Without these exchanges, engagement does not happen in the first place! The social aspect encouraged by EAG membership is unparalleled. We get to meet people of similar interests, and to work on small projects to promote those interests. This is quite inspiring.

"Also, I also have to add to the point raised both by Brian and Antonio on job efficiency. Sometimes it is challenging to be active in the group amidst our workload. EAG activities are additional tasks in our To-Do lists at work. We remind ourselves that our advocacies should not distract us from our day jobs, so to speak. We are bank employees first, EAG members next," Alice explains.

Brian said, "If you are going to ask me as the company's CEO the question 'does the program work?' I'd say yes, it does. To date, there are 6,300 GBC employees who are members of our nine action groups. This demonstrates that we have 6,300 employees who want to do more at work apart from their usual job descriptions. A very good sign of an engaged employee base. Moreover, our industry peers have recognized our effort in promoting organisational inclusion and diversity. We have set benchmarks for this area. Your Welcome Kit lists awards that the company won in relation to this."

Lily quickly checked the list and saw the following awards:

- 2015 Australian Human Resources Institute's (AHRI) "Most Inclusive Workplace" Award
- ABLE won the AHRI 2014 Disability Employment Award and 2013 National Disability Award for Excellence in Employment Outcomes
- GLOBAL won the Best LGBTI Network Award
- CEO (BT Financial Group) was recognized as Executive Sponsor of the Year at the 2015 Australian Workplace Equality Index Awards
- 2014 Best Employer International for 50+ Employees

Lily thought the EAGs were fascinating! She has yet to hear stories from her friends' work experiences that are similar to this.

Toward the end of the program, Brian read the statement that he wrote in the "Taking Action" report, "My starting point when talking about diversity is to say, 'This is a business issue.' It might be a happy coincidence that there are social justice outcomes as well, but actually you can be totally commercial about this and say that a more diverse and inclusive workforce means we can get better quality people working for us. It means we make more thoughtful and insightful decisions and therefore do better over time. Thank you. Welcome again to GBC."

Lily found the whole Orientation Day program informative and inspiring. It made her feel that she will be valued as an employee at GBC.

Olami queried, "Will you join an action group eventually?"

Lily answered, "I might. I am really inclined to meet other people from other divisions or departments. I think this is important for me as I settle into the workplace. In my previous work, I did not socialize enough with colleagues. For one, the culture of the place did not emphasize socialization the way GBC seems to be espousing."

Zihen cheerfully added, "We might see each other in one of the groups then; we'll never know!"

The three of them exchanged contact numbers. After that, they bid each other good-bye. On her way out of the venue after the program, Lily posted on Twitter: *Happy to be celebrated here in my new workplace. #newbeginnings #proudnewbie*

She could not wait for Monday, her first official day at work.

DISCUSSION QUESTIONS

1. What skillsets are necessary for employees to thrive in a multicultural or diverse workplace?
2. What challenges do communication divergences in the workplace create?
3. What is the connection between promoting organizational diversity and organizational effectiveness? What is the *dis*connect?

4. Discuss the relationship between socialization processes and organizational diversity.
5. From a newcomer socialization perspective, discuss why an orientation program benefits new employees.
6. In what ways does joining small groups or teams in the workplace become an information-seeking strategy for employees?

SUGGESTED READINGS

Acker, J. (2006). Inequality regimes: Gender, class, and race in organizations. *Gender & Society, 20*, 441-464.

Chung, J. (2001). *The challenge of diversity in global organization: Communication and global society.* New York, NY: Peter Lang.

Diversity Council of Australia. [Report.] *Taking action.* (2015). Retrieved from https://www.westpac.com.au/content/dam/public/wbc/documents/pdf/aw/Inclusion%20and%20Diversity/DCA_Case_Study_Westpac%20Online_Final.pdf

Macnamara, J. (2016). *Organizational listening: The missing essential in public communication.* New York, NY: Peter Lang.

Macnamara, J. (2018). Toward a theory and practice of organizational listening. *International Journal of Listening, 32*, 1–23.

Muchiri, M., & Ayoko, O. (2013). Linking demographic diversity to organisational outcomes. *Leadership and Organisational Development Journal, 34*, 384–406.

Shen, J., Chanda, A., D'Netto, B., & Monga, M. (2009). Managing diversity through human resource management: An international perspective and conceptual framework. *The International Journal of Human Resource Management, 20*, 235–251.

MUSIC IS ALL I KNOW—A SPECIAL CASE OF ANTICIPATORY ROLE SOCIALIZATION?

Elena Gabor, PhD
Bradley University

"What are you getting for dinner, guys? I think I'm getting a pizza and a salad," said Andrew.

"You must be hungry," remarked Jennifer.

"Well, I've been in that practice room for 2 hours! I need to get the music into my fingers for the Brahms recital coming in 2 months. I'm starved!" Andrew replied.

Jennifer, David, Andrew, and Elaine were high school seniors and members of the Youth Symphony in Midwest City. They were all 18, with an air of maturity beyond their years. The first month of their senior year had just ended.

"So, have you started your college applications?" asked David. "How are the essays coming?"

All three of his friends kept looking at their plates.

"Mine is almost done," said Andrew. "I am still working on it, though. But it's the audition I'm most worried about. I just read an article about a percussionist auditioning for a major orchestra, who experienced the unthinkable: He dropped the sticks!"

This chapter is based on published work: Gabor, E. (2013). 'Tuning' the body of the classical musician: An embodied approach to vocational anticipatory socialization. *Qualitative Research in Organizations and Management—An International Journal*, 8(3), 206–223.

"Oh, wow! That would be catastrophic, indeed. But it happens, you know?" replied David.

"I'm not even sure what to do," said Jennifer. "All I've known in my life is music! Really, it's all I know! In a perfect world, I'd major in Viola Performance and that's it. But I think I'll need a plan B or something in order to make it. I think I'll end up doing Physical Therapy and Viola Performance."

"Come on, we all know your true love is viola!" remarked David. "What do you know about physical therapy?"

"I know a little since I needed physical therapy for my bow hand recently. And it pays well, with benefits!" smiled Jennifer.

"It's not gonna be easy, you know, to pursue two majors with all the recitals, rehearsals, and concerts that Performance students do," said Andrew, with an air of wisdom. "But if anyone can do it, it's you."

"Yeah, I know, and thanks. I just don't want to put all my eggs in one basket," said Jennifer. "What if I don't make it? Or what if I marry and have kids and we need more income? A musician's life is not easy."

"Well, I've made up my mind: I'm going to major in Piano and Conducting," said David to move the conversation along. "I'll apply at the Cleveland Institute. If I get accepted, I'll get a free ride!"

"Yeah, it makes sense," remarked Andrew. "You conducted us pretty well when Maestro gave you the baton last semester in the youth symphony. You better start work on that audition!"

"Thanks, bud," smiled David. "I already started working on it with my teacher. How about you? Have you decided on a major yet?"

"Yes, of course! Music Ed!" replied Andrew without hesitation. "Somebody's gotta teach this, no?"

"Well, those who can't do it, teach!" joked Elaine.

Andrew did not mind. He had everyone's respect in the room because he played four instruments—clarinet, violin, percussion, and piano—and played them well. He had the scar of violinists on the left side of his neck, a sign that he practiced regularly and a "badge of honor" for violinists. They all had a sense that Andrew would grow up to be an awesome orchestra or band teacher like Mr. Johnson at their high school, whom everyone loved.

They all sat down with their food trays and ate quietly for a while.

"You haven't told us about your plans, Elaine," remarked Andrew. "Have you chosen a major yet? What's it going to be?"

"Still not sure, but I'm leaning towards Cello Performance and Speech Therapy," answered Elaine with a straight face. "I trust my cello skills, but want a plan B, too."

"That's interesting," commented David. He wondered why his female musician friends thought about complicating their student lives with double majors, while his male musician friends seemed much more confident in their future and didn't seem to care about plan Bs. Maybe the girls were more cautious for a reason he still needed to understand, or they took longer to grow confidence in themselves.

"Really, guys, if we think about it, how many years of serious classical music training do we have between us? I started in piano at age 4 and now I'm 18. I have 14 years of daily practice under my belt. I gave my first public recital at age 5 and had my first competition at 7. How about you, Jennifer?"

The energy at the table went up noticeably.

"I started in violin when I was 5, then I moved to viola at 10. So, yeah, 8 solid years of viola," replied Jennifer.

"How about you, Andrew?" asked David.

"Well, let me think: I started in piano at 4, violin at 5, clarinet at 9, and percussion at 11. I feel like I've been reading, playing, and composing music all my life!"

Andrew knew everyone in town who was involved in music in one way or another. He had been playing wedding gigs since the age of 13 and teaching young children in his studio since he was in 10th grade.

"Yeah, it's like you don't even need to go to college! You're a professional musician already!" said Elaine. Her smile disappeared quickly, as she sensed that that was close to the reality as Andrew perceived it. For him, the high school activities almost got in the way of his musical work. On the other side of the table, David had an interesting story, too. Two major newspapers had labeled him a prodigy at age 11 when he performed a piano concerto with the professional orchestra in the nearby city. The local TV channel made a story about him when he was only in sixth grade. He even got accepted at Juilliard's pre-college division, but decided not to attend.

"How about you, Elaine?" asked David.

"I got started in Suzuki violin when I was 6 and in cello when I was 8. Once I discovered the cello, I never looked back. So, 10 years for me." Elaine also had a private studio where she taught cello to six elementary and middle school students.

Another moment of silence passed while the four chewed their food and sipped from their drinks, their gazes fixed on the hands of the person in front of them. Four pairs of expert hands—with thin, long, and muscular fingers, with visible blue veins and thin wrists. Hands with sensitive calluses, expert in vibrato, rhythm, and pressure. Parents, grandparents, and private teachers had advised these young musicians throughout their childhoods not to play rough sports. David started tapping the table as if he was keying numbers in a calculator. For a second, others thought he was mentally practicing a piano piece, which he did often in the cafeteria.

"Okay," said David, "so that makes what, almost 40 years of serious training for all of us together?"

"Wow! Never thought of it that way," remarked Andrew. "My cousin is just now wondering what major to pursue and finding out what he is interested in, but for me, I've known since sixth grade: I'm a musician! My parents never had to send me to practice since, because for me it's like brushing my teeth!"

"I feel the same way, you know?" said Jennifer. "My identity has been that of a musician very early in my life, which makes my college decision even harder, because my mom is telling me *not* to become a professional musician. She says often that 'music is great, but a career in music is not.' She tells me to get a 'real job' and become an orthodontist, or marry one (here Jennifer revealed her braces in an exaggerated smile), because then I'll have money for good instruments!"

The others laughed knowingly, but only for a brief 2 seconds, their faces becoming serious again. If there was ever a hug made of gentle gazes, their faces hugged Jennifer in that moment. They all knew Jennifer's mom was a freelance violinist struggling to make it in their midsize town, always with concert attire in the trunk, putting a lot of miles on her car to travel to nearby cities to perform.

"Don't worry, I got the same message from my folks," said David. "They told me to think twice, that a musical career is hard and all that, but I told them: 'Mom, Dad, how do you expect me to not want music to be my life, when you guys have raised me in the orchestra pit, music is all you guys talk about at the dinner table, and our family's happiest moments involve music one way or another?' So, they may have told me not to become a musician, but they've shown me the opposite. I don't think they have the slightest idea how contradictory their messages have been!"

"You know," Andrew intervened, "I choose to look at the positive side of things. Yes, a freelance career like your mom's, Jennifer, or my dad's, is hard, but, in my opinion, the '08 crisis made a lot of people look at freelance musicians to learn how to make it in the new gigging economy. Moonlighting is a lot of people's career model now, it seems. I, for one, am proud of the resilience I've learned from my dad," said Andrew with a serious tone of voice.

"Yeah, but God forbid our parents get injured and can't play!" said Jennifer.

After 10 deafening seconds of silence, David changed the topic:

"Recently, Stacey, a new neighbor of mine, told me how grateful she was that she moved into a community like ours with lots of musical organizations and events like our regional orchestra, our youth symphony, Music in the Park, or the Jazz Band. She had little idea how many of those groups survive thanks to volunteer work, but she definitely appreciates the talent that is here," said David.

"Yeah, my mom volunteers a lot to maintain her professional contacts. A fifth of her gigs are not paid, but she likes the work and the people she gets to work with," said Jennifer. "Plus, she appreciates the flexibility her schedule affords her. But she also had situations where she expected to be paid, and those hiring her expected her to play for free, out of her love of music. I wish more people understood that it takes years of disciplined work to build a stage-worthy level of performance and that it should be rewarded properly," said Jennifer.

"Unfortunately, often audiences can't tell the difference between amateur and professional musicians," added David. "Look at our own orchestra. It sounds okay for most ears in the audience, but how many people see the folks in the back chairs who can't yet do vibrato or fake their way through the hard parts? I know an orchestra is not a surgical team; if somebody makes a mistake, it's not the end of the world, and yet, as artists, we are trained to play close to perfection!"

Always the optimist in the group, Andrew jumped in with a cheerful tone: "That's why I'm going to Midwest College, where Mr. Smith teaches. Remember how, at music camp last year, he made us play in the dark? He turned off all the lights and told us to play not just with our minds, but with our bodies, too! He was all about the mind-body unity and the distributed musical memory and all that."

"Yeah, Mr. Smith is great. He's quite the mentor!" agreed David.

Andrew finished his food and noticed everyone else had finished, too. He collected everyone's trash and put the trays away.

"On this note, I need to get going. Keep your chins up, guys, we'll all be fine." Then in sotto voce, he sounded the notes from *Finding Nemo*: "'Just keep swimming, just keep swimming!'"

Everyone laughed. "Yeah, bud, you bet!" said David. "Take care."

They all rose from their chairs, hugged each other, picked up their instrument cases, and left the cafeteria. On his way home, David kept reflecting on the experiences of family members and musician friends who started serious, disciplined work in childhood. Society continues to see childhood as a play time, but, he thought, for musicians, athletes, and ballet dancers, childhood is filled with hard work. He also thought about how the instruments "wrote" on his body with scars, calluses, aural abilities, knowledge, and memories. At 18, he had the fully formed mind-body unity of a musician. As he entered his living room and saw diplomas and pictures of performances with nationally known artists and orchestras, he thought to himself how lucky he had been. He then sat down at the piano, started the metronome, stretched his hands, fixed his posture, and opened the music book to practice for his college audition.

DISCUSSION QUESTIONS

1. Do you agree that the occupational role identity of classical musicians, dancers, athletes, and other embodied occupations may form earlier in life than that of non-musicians, nondancers, and nonathletes? Why? Why not? Further, can their professional careers start before age 18?

2. What are some forces influencing the anticipatory role socialization of classical musicians that are mentioned in this case?

3. From what you have observed, how does the media portray classical musicians today?

4. In the case, one student mentions that verbal socialization messages and socialization messages from the media and environment can be contradictory. If you were or are a musician, athlete, or dancer, and you have been the recipient of such contradictory messages, how did you make sense of them for your own career choice?

5. Can one's mind-body unity be considered a source of anticipatory role socialization along with family, media, school, and other sources?

SUGGESTED READINGS

Bamberger, J. (2006). What develops in musical development? In G. E. McPherson (Ed.), *The child as musician: A handbook of musical development* (pp. 69–92). New York, NY: Oxford University Press.

Gabor, E. (2013). 'Tuning' the body of the classical musician: An embodied approach to vocational anticipatory socialization. *Qualitative Research in Organizations and Management—An International Journal, 8*, 206–223. doi:10.1108/QROM-05-2012-1068.

Gabor, E. (2011). Turning points in the development of classical musicians. *Journal of Ethnographic and Qualitative Research, 5*, 138–156.

Johnson, M. (2007). *The meaning of the body. Aesthetics of human understanding.* Chicago, IL: University of Chicago Press.

Levitine, D. (2007). *This is your brain on music. The science of a human obsession.* New York, NY: Penguin Group.

Manturzewska, M. (1990). A biographical study of the life-span development of professional musicians. *Psychology of Music, 18*, 112–139.

Sloboda, J., & Howe, M. (1992). Transitions in the early musical careers of able young musicians: Choosing instruments and teachers. *Journal of Research in Music Education, 40*(3), 283–294.

LEARNING TO ROCK THE BOAT WHEN A SUPERVISOR MISSTEPS

Natalie Nelson-Marsh, PhD
University of Portland

Vanessa sighed and rubbed her hands together as she waited in the hallway for her turn. "It's going to be okay." Greg assured her, "It's only another simulation. How hard can it be?" But even as he said this to Vanessa, he felt the anticipation growing. They walked silently down the hallway in their scrubs toward their next nursing practicum simulation. They have been practicing administering care using life-size robotic mannequins. Everyone in their nursing program at the University enjoyed these simulations—other than the notorious "supervisor-subordinate conflict" simulation. Rumor had it that standing up to a supervisor nurse or doctor making a medical mistake was extremely uncomfortable, *even* during a simulation with a robotic patient.

"What was it Dr. Jorgenson said in class about nursing distress and burnout?" Greg asked Vanessa.

"She said that it isn't the nursing work itself that causes distress and burnout. Distress emerges in situations where you know the ethically correct choice to make, but feel constrained and powerless to act on

This chapter is based on consulting experiences and published work: Krautscheid, L., Luebbering, C., & Krautscheid, B. A. (2017). Conflict-handling styles demonstrated by nursing students in response to microethical dilemmas. *Nursing Education Perspectives, 38*, 143–145.

your convictions. It is the regularity of feeling powerless when dealing with micro-ethical dilemmas that leads to a steady state of distress," Vanessa recounted.

"Well, I definitely don't want to become the one nurse out of three who leaves his position due to burnout," Greg responded. "So, I guess I'd rather practice dealing with micro-ethical dilemmas now in order to learn how to navigate conflict with our supervisors later."

Yet Greg understood Vanessa's worry and knew this simulation would be uncomfortable. It would move beyond managing intravenous lines and administering medication. "*What will I say to my supervisor in the moment? How do I advocate for a patient and myself when a senior nurse or doctor missteps?*" he wondered.

Greg and Vanessa reached the simulation hospital room and found their professor, Dr. Jorgenson, waiting for them. She offered a friendly wave.

Without wasting any time, Dr. Jorgenson began her description of the simulation. "Alright, I know that this simulation is a bit different so let me provide an overview of your assignment today. Your patient is an elderly woman who has a wound on her left foot that is infected. The wound needs to be cultured, and the patient needs to be monitored closely. You can expect that a senior nurse will be working with both of you on this case, and she will make some sort of medical error. You need to advocate for the patient and change the course of care provided, mitigating the error while also preserving your professional relationship with your supervisor. Any questions?"

Greg and Vanessa both shook their heads no. Vanessa glanced at Greg with wide eyes.

"OK then, you're on." Dr. Jorgenson held the door open and ushered them in with an encouraging smile.

The Simulation Begins

As Vanessa and Greg entered the hospital room, everything was as they expected. The light-green walls, the white tile floor, the monitors beeping, computer screens displaying vitals, and the beloved robotic patient they had named Noelle was in bed. Vanessa moved toward the head of the bed and began reading the monitor. There was a knock at the door.

"Come in," Greg said pleasantly. "*Here we go*," he thought.

Jane, the senior nurse, entered the room in her white coat over scrubs, took a glob of hand sanitizer from the dispenser by the door, and smiled as she walked toward the bed rubbing her hands together. "Hi, I'm Jane."

"Hi, Jane." Greg and Vanessa responded in unison.

"So, today our patient needs a wound culture, right? And this is Noelle Johnson, right?" Jane asked as she nodded to their robotic patient.

Greg answered, "Yes, but she's not very responsive at the moment."

Jane reached deep into her white coat pocket, looked down, and spoke absently to her patient. "Hi Noelle, I'm here to take your wound culture." While fumbling with latex gloves she retrieved from her pocket, Jane mumbled, "Alright let's see. Let's get her wound culture in so we can start the antibiotics." But, as Jane pulled on the gloves, she exclaimed, "Oh my goodness!"

"Oh, did you rip your glove?" Greg asked as he walked back to the end of the bed. He was facing Jane.

Jane, working to pull off the ripped glove, sighed, "Yeah. I forgot to trim my nails this morning." Vanessa laughed nervously and Jane continued, "Well, whatever, it's a wound culture, it's supposed to be dirty so . . ." She trailed off and moved to take the culture without a sterile glove on her hand.

Greg stepped toward Jane and said, "I'm going to have to ask you to get another glove. There's one right over there." He pointed toward the glove dispenser behind Jane.

Jane looked up at Greg, paused, and smiled. He stood silently and waited for her to replace the glove. Jane glanced behind her and around the room, her hands hovering over the patient's wounded foot. "God. Would you get it for me?" she asked Greg. But before he could answer, Jane relented with slight irritation, "Ah. Fine. I'll get it."

"Thanks," Greg responded and turned back toward the computer with Vanessa. He and Vanessa made eye contact and both smiled timidly.

Jane walked over and grabbed a new glove from the dispenser on the wall. "Thank you for telling me because I am rushing. I have so many things to do, you know?"

Greg smiled and nodded. "Yeah, yeah. It's just important to go slow. You don't want to . . . " but he trailed off unsure of what to say next.

Jane looked up, made eye contact, and said assertively, "You're right, I don't want to infect myself, right?"

Slightly stunned, Greg faced Jane. "Or," he paused. "Or the person. Even worse," he said as he pointed to and looked at Noelle in bed.

Jane agreed, "Or her." In silence, she looked down and began to open the culture cotton swab. Jane leaned over to examine the wound on the patient's foot. She took the long cotton swab and concentrated on dabbing it gently on the patient's foot wound. She then placed the cotton swab back into its original paper packaging.

Greg's body jolted. He leaned forward, watching Jane intently. "Aren't you supposed to put the cotton swab into a tube and not back into the paper packaging?" He rubbed his hands together, anxiously. He cracked his knuckles.

Jane looked up from her bent-over position at Noelle's foot. She did not smile. She resisted. "Yes. But this packaging is sterile enough. I'm just going straight to the lab down the hall after I leave." She cocked her head to the right and did not smile as she looked at Greg.

Greg continued, "It may be sterile enough, but that is not standard practice. There is a special container that you put wound cultures in. It's a tube, right Vanessa?" He made a twisting motion with his hands as if he had an invisible tube to demonstrate. He looked to Vanessa for confirmation and support.

"Yeah, a little culture tube thing," Vanessa added, nodding her head, looking first to Greg and then back at Jane.

Greg nodded in agreement with Vanessa, grateful for her support. "Yeah," he smiled nervously. "A culture tube."

Jane tilted her head and looked at Greg. She shrugged her shoulders. "We have tubes to keep the culture sterile," she lectured. Her body posture changed from relaxed to tense. She leaned on one leg, hip jutted out, head tilted to the side as she stated, "But this is also sterile packaging."

Greg interrupted gently asking, "Do you not have the tube for it?"

"No, I don't have the tube with me," Jane responded, deadpan.

Greg persisted. "You kind of need to do it over because it's not good now." His face reddened.

"Well, I don't have it now."

"Could you come back with the tube?"

After a brief pause, Jane replied. "Yeah, I would have to come back. But I mean, I have done this before and no one has said anything."

"Yeah, well, we are saying something now." As Greg said this, he faced Jane, smiled, and laughed a little.

"I'll have to go check the policy because no one has really said anything before. But thank you for telling me. I will double check." Jane responded, softening.

"That would be awesome. That would be great."

Jane let out a sigh, "I am not sure when I can come back. I'll see how booked I am. Okay?"

Greg answered with a quiet "Sure."

As Jane moves toward the door, she said, "I'll call you and let you know when I can come back" and left the room.

The Aftermath

After the door closed, Vanessa and Greg let their shoulders drop. Greg felt exhausted.

Vanessa shook her head and said, "Well, I'm sorry I completely failed you. I just didn't know what to say."

Greg's face felt hot. "It's okay. That was hard." He thought to himself for a minute and then said considerately, "Okay, so the simulation wasn't a real-world experience, but we are learning from someone else's real-world story. That was a simulation, but it felt very, very real. I think now we will be better at noticing what is going on in the moment and know that we need to respond. We can't bend our standards because the little decisions we make in the moment matter. What we say and what we do will have a big impact in the lives of our patients."

DISCUSSION QUESTIONS

1. How do simulations like this one aid in anticipatory role socialization for under-graduate nursing students who can expect to deal regularly with uncomfortable moments and ethical challenges?
2. What are the implications of training members to expect difficult coworker inter-actions?
3. Research shows that nurses experience burnout not because of the stress of daily work, but due to difficult communication situations that require confronting su-pervisors and peers. What makes these situations so challenging?
4. Current research also highlights that nursing practitioners benefit greatly from peer communication when dealing with difficult communication experiences. Please explain how and why peer communication could reduce burnout.
5. How might emotions play an important role for nurses when faced with an ethi-cally charged interaction?
6. When might other organizational newcomers—from student interns to new employees—face similar decisions about confronting supervisors who are not fol-lowing the rules? How important is it to follow the rules and standard practices when there is not an immediate threat?

SUGGESTED READINGS

American Association of Colleges and Nursing. (2008). Moral distress position state-ment. *AACN Public Policy.* Retrieved from http://aacn.org/moraldistresspossition.

Bisel, R. S., Kelley, K. M., Ploeger, N. A., & Messersmith, J. (2011). Workers' moral mum effect: On facework and unethical behavior in the workplace. *Communication Studies, 62,* 153–170.

Jameton, A. (1984). *Nursing practice: The ethical issues.* Englewood Cliffs, NJ: Prentice-Hall.

Krautscheid, L., Luebbering, C., & Krautscheid, B. A. (2017). Conflict-handling styles demonstrated by nursing students in response to microethical dilemmas. *Nursing Education Perspectives, 38,* 143–145.

LEARNING THAT "NURSES EAT THEIR YOUNG"

5

ENCOUNTERING INTERGENERATIONAL CONFLICT IN THE WORKPLACE

Lindsey B. Anderson, PhD
University of Maryland

Melanie Morgan, PhD
Purdue University

Emma took a deep breath as she stood outside of Anne's office. It was her first day working at Local Hospital as a registered nurse (RN). She had just graduated from nursing school the week before and was excited to have a job in the pediatric unit. Emma was scheduled to meet with Anne, the Director of Nursing (DON), at 6:45 a.m.—15 minutes before she was to start her first shift, but Anne was running late.

The feeling of excitement started to fade as the minutes ticked by. Emma thought about all she learned over the years at school while she waited in the hallway. Besides knowing how to monitor a patient's blood pressure, administer medicine, and communicate with patients, she was also taught to be wary of her older colleagues. She remembered one of her instructor's warnings, "Remember, nurses eat their young."

When one of her friends asked if that was true, the instructor responded by simply stating, "With salt and pepper," as if it were common knowledge. Those comments stuck with Emma.

This chapter is based on published work: Anderson, L. B., & Morgan, M. (2017). Do nurses eat their young?: Understanding nurses' intergenerational communicative experiences in the workplace. *Communication Quarterly*, 65, 377–401. doi:http://dx.doi.org/10.1080/014633 73.2016.1259175

Emma then remembered the horror stories that were shared in class discussions. She recalled one of her classmates, Lauren, saying, "My sister, Leigh, is a nurse and she told me to be careful because the older nurses are domineering and judgmental."

Emma wanted to know more, so she asked, "Really? What do they do?"

Lauren continued her story, "Well, one time Leigh asked an older nurse to help her change a patient's port because she was having trouble, and the nurse rolled her eyes and told Leigh to figure it out herself because she had her own patients to take care of."

Anne finally appeared with a cup of coffee in her hand, bringing Emma back to reality. Anne unlocked the door to the DON office and stepped inside without saying a word.

Emma took another deep breath and followed Anne into the office. She thought, *"The stories can't be true. Nurses couldn't really eat their young. The warnings have to be exaggerated."*

Anne made her way back to a large desk covered in stacks of paper and sat in a rolling chair as she looked up at Emma, giving her a forced smile.

"Well, Emma," Anne said as she gestured for Emma to sit in one of the two small chairs that were positioned in front of the desk, "I'm going to give you the same speech I give to all the new girls." Anne cleared her throat and continued, "This is a tough job; it's taxing and it's hard—not at all like it is portrayed on television or in movies. It's more than walking around the halls in cute little scrubs and flirting with the doctors. It's blood, sweat, and tears. Are you really ready to be a nurse?"

Emma gulped; she was caught off guard. She expected Anne to welcome her to the unit, not to tell her how tough the job was or to minimize her passion for caring for others. Emma thought, *"I always wanted to be a nurse; why is she saying these patronizing things to me?"* Then she replied, "Yes, I am ready and I plan to work hard. I did a great job in my clinicals . . ."

Anne interrupted Emma, "We'll see about that."

Then there was a knock on the door and Anne waved in another nurse. Anne introduced Emma to Susan, the most senior nurse on the pediatric unit and Emma's point of contact during her first shift.

* * * * *

Emma and Susan left Anne's office just ahead of 7:00 a.m. Emma tried to start a conversation, "So how long have you been here?"

Susan replied, "20 years and I have been training young nurses like you since Anne became the DON in 2010. It is tough getting you all up to speed. Your generation needs so much additional training and direction."

"What do you mean?" Emma retorted. "I just completed nursing school and learned so much during my clinicals. I am up to date on all the newest procedures and hospital technology."

Susan scoffed. "That doesn't mean you're a good nurse or that you know what you're doing. I suggest you pay attention to the way we do things here and listen to the veteran nurses like me and Anne."

Susan then stopped in front of the nurses' station and motioned for Emma to enter the large, rectangular, shared desk space.

"Okay, since you're so well trained, I have an easy task for you," Susan said as she took a seat in front of a computer. "Just get the shift report for each of our patients from Rachel before she leaves. You will need to review each file and organize them so we can start our rounds." She turned around and with a few clicks of the keyboard, starting checking her email.

* * * * *

Once Emma finished reviewing the shift reports and summarized them for Susan, they started their rounds. First, they made their way to an empty patient room that was directly across from the nurses' station.

"Okay, the patient who stayed in this room was discharged last night. We need to get it ready for any incoming patients." Susan paused and looked at her Apple watch. "I'm going to get a cup of coffee while you change the soiled sheets and discard any medical waste that has not already been picked up."

Emma hesitated, "Shouldn't the orderlies or CNAs do this for us? I thought this type of work was part of their job."

Susan rolled her eyes. "We all help where we can on this unit." She then turned toward the door and over her shoulder said, "I'll be back in a few minutes."

Emma watched Susan leave and then sighed as she gathered the bed linens.

* * * * *

Next, Susan and Emma went to another patient room. Susan said, "Please put in an IV for this patient. I need to run across the hall and talk to some worried parents."

Emma said timidly, "Okay," and walked into the room.

Emma greeted the patient, a school-aged boy who was dehydrated following a case of influenza. She prepped the IV bag and tubing easily while making small talk with the family.

"You are my first patient," Emma said to the boy. He smiled weakly at her in response.

His mother looked up from her phone and asked, "You mean your first patient of the day, right?"

"No," Emma said quickly, "this is my first day as an official RN. I just graduated last week."

Emma then started the process of inserting the patient's IV, but she struggled to find a vein with the needle. She felt sweat prick at her forehead and felt her hands start to shake.

The boy's mother noticed, too, and asked sharply, "Are you sure you know what you are doing? Do you need another nurse to help you?"

Then Susan entered the room and, in an exasperated voice, said, "Come on, Emma; you should know how to do this. I'm sure prepping an IV bag was covered in your clinicals."

Then Susan grabbed the needle from Emma, found the vein effortlessly, and hung the IV bag. She then turned to the mother and apologized for Emma. "I'm sorry about that. I will keep a closer eye on Emma. If you need anything, ask for me."

The mother, still not pleased, thanked Susan and inquired when the doctor would be in to give her an update on her son.

But at this point, Emma wasn't listening. She was dumbfounded and watched the interaction with her mouth agape. She couldn't believe that Susan just did that to her, especially in front of a patient and his family. She was mortified. Emma needed to gather herself, so she turned around and hurried out of the patient's room.

* * * * *

Emma found a bathroom. She pushed open the door and made her way to the sink to splash water on her face. Then she heard a flush. Emma turned around to see another woman in scrubs looking at her.

"Hi, I'm Chloe. You must be Emma. I heard you were joining our unit today."

Chloe grabbed a couple of towels and handed them to Emma so she could dry her dripping face. "Let me guess—Susan is showing you the ropes today. I shadowed her during my first day. I drove away in tears and swore I would never come back, but I did."

Chloe sighed and patted Emma on the shoulder. "I know the older nurses can be mean. They are such bullies—always looking to criticize us or embarrass us, especially in front of patients and their families."

Emma sniffled. "I just don't understand. Why do they act like this?"

"I don't know," Chloe responded with a sympathetic look. "I wish I could say it gets better, but it hasn't for me—you just get used to it." Chloe continued. "I looked into transferring to a different unit, but I heard that the climate isn't any better."

Emma nodded, feeling disappointed and second-guessing her career choice. This was not what she expected.

"Well, I need to go. Let me know if you need anything—even just to vent," Chloe added as she turned to walk out of the restroom.

Emma looked at herself in the mirror. She had calmed down and was ready to get back out on the floor.

As she threw away the paper towel she used to dry her face, she reflected on what Chloe had said, the actions of her older colleagues, and the warnings she received in nursing school. *"Why would older nurses purposefully eat their young? Is it a rite of passage? A form of hazing? Part of the culture?"* Emma wasn't sure, but she knew one thing, she would remember this feeling and vowed to never eat her young . . . if she stayed in nursing.

DISCUSSION QUESTIONS

1. Describe the boundaries (functional, hierarchical, and inclusionary) that Emma encountered on her first day at the hospital.
2. How should Emma attempt to reduce the uncertainty (task and relational) that she experiences as an organizational newcomer?
3. Which socialization strategies were demonstrated in Emma's story? Make sure to describe the socialization strategies in terms of context, patterns, and goals.
4. Describe the conflict illustrated through this case study in terms of level, content, and visibility.
5. If you were in Emma's position, how would you address the conflict?

SUGGESTED READINGS

Anderson, L. B., & Morgan, M. (2017). Do nurses eat their young?: Understanding nurses' intergenerational communicative experiences in the workplace. *Communication Quarterly, 65*, 377–401. doi:http://dx.doi.org/10.1080/01463373.2016.1259175

Dailey, S. L. (2016). I'm new ... again: Reconceptualizing the socialization process through rotational programs. *Communication Studies, 67*, 183–208. doi:10.1080/10510974.2016.1145130

Hewett, D. G., Watson, B. M., Gallois, C., Ward, M., & Leggett, B. A. (2009). Intergroup communication between hospital doctors: Implications for quality of patient care. *Social Science & Medicine, 69*, 1732–1740. doi:10.1016/j.socscimed.2009.09.048

Hummert, M. L., Garstka, T. A., Bonneson, J. L., & Strahm, S. (1994). Stereotypes of the elderly held by the young, middle-aged, and elderly adults. *Journal of Gerontology, 49*, 240–249. doi:10.1093/geronj/49.5.P240

McCann, R. M., & Giles, H. (2006). Communication with people of different ages in the workplace: Thai and American data. *Human Communication Research, 32*, 74–108. doi:10.1111/j.1468-2958.2006.00004.x

Myers, K. K., & Sadaghiani, K. (2010). Millennials in the workplace: A communication perspective on Millennials' organizational relationships and performance. *Journal of Business Psychology, 25*, 225–238. doi:10.1007/s10869-010-9172-7

Stephens, K. K., & Dailey, S. L. (2012). Situated organizational identification in newcomers: Impacts of pre-entry organizational exposure. *Management Communication Quarterly, 26*, 404–422. doi:10.1177/0893318912440179

LEAVING COLLEGE FOR THE "FAST TRACK"

ASSIMILATION EXPERIENCES OF MULTIPLE TRANSITIONS

Angie Pastorek, PhD
University of Kansas, Edwards Campus

Angela Gist-Mackey, PhD
University of Kansas

Sam Rivera, a 19-year-old freshman, earned a coveted spot as a business major at Big State U. He knew he was lucky—most potential business majors started at Big State U as an "undeclared" major and hoped to secure a spot in the "B-School" during their junior year.

Sam thrived, taking a full 15-hour course load and working as a part-time events coordinator for the Tomlinson School of Business. Sam loved working, always had—on his 15th birthday, he asked his mom to drive him around to apply for jobs. He also knew his working-class parents sacrificed to save for his tuition, room, and board. Now, he took great pride in helping to pay for his own monthly expenses, while saving 30% of every paycheck. His mother always reminded him about the importance of "saving up for the unexpected."

He loved the networking opportunities that came with working in the B-school—regularly chatting with influential alumni and business leaders who spoke at B-school events. That's how Sam met Ken Tomlinson, entrepreneur and CEO of Drive U, a rapidly expanding local chain of driving schools based in Dallas. Sam met Ken when he

This chapter is based on dissertation research: Pastorek. A. E. (2015). *Organizational exit dynamics in times of turbulence: Let me tell you the story of how my high hopes were let down* (Unpublished doctoral dissertation). The University of Texas, Austin, Texas.

visited the popular Entrepreneurship 780 class for MBA students. Ken was the son of a wealthy Texas family and a Big State U "Distinguished Alumni," an honor reserved for alums who achieved the pinnacle of business success, were well connected across the state, and were generous donors to Big State U.

Sam managed to sneak into the MBA class for Ken's talk shortly after it began. Ken's dynamic speaking style captivated Sam. He regaled the MBA students with stories of the fast-paced, complex nature of an entrepreneurial venture. Sam knew he had to grab a few minutes of Ken's time to ask about Drive U's summer internship program. While he could hardly contain his excitement, Sam waited patiently for 45 minutes while Ken chatted with professors and MBA students after his presentation.

Ken had seen Sam at the back of the room.

"Hey there, guy," Ken said. "What's your name?"

Sam came down the aisle, looked Ken in the eye, and offered a firm handshake, "Hi, Mr. Tomlinson. My name is Samuel Rivera. I'm a freshman here in the B-School—I'm taking intro classes in entrepreneurship. I worked in the driving school industry back home in San Antonio for a year and a half. I see exactly what you were talking about tonight—there is huge opportunity in the market since there's no national chain of driving schools."

"Wow, you've done your homework, Sam." Ken was clearly impressed by Sam's industry knowledge. "My team has been researching where we should expand first. What are your thoughts?"

Sam shared a number of details highlighting why Houston was the biggest potential market based on its rapidly expanding population of families with high school children and high number of first-generation immigrant families settling in the area. Sam was shocked by what Ken said next.

"Impressive, Sam. I haven't announced this publicly, but I'm opening two new locations in Houston this summer. And I still need someone to manage the main one in the Heights neighborhood—not only day-to-day operations, but also further developing our expansion plans for the Houston market. It's an once-in-a-lifetime opportunity. You're clearly a bright guy. I'd love to have you join the team. What do you say?"

Sam was stunned. "Wow, thank you, Mr. Tomlinson. I would love to work with you. I'm not sure how my parents would feel about me taking this on while in school, though. I'd love to join you for a summer internship from May through August."

"Like I said, it's a once-in-a-lifetime opportunity, Sam. I'd need you full-time for the foreseeable future. We can start working on the expansion plans while you finish out this semester, and then you can come live with my wife and me at our condo in Houston this summer while you launch the Heights location. Rent-free. Take the weekend to think about it, check with your parents, and let me know. I really need someone who can eventually step into the CEO role—and I can see you have that potential. School will always be here; I took a year off to help my dad with the family business and came back to finish school later on. This is a rare opportunity—and a bright kid like you can surely find a way to make it all work."

Sam went back to his dorm that night and Skyped with his parents. They had saved for years for his tuition and were incredibly proud to have their only son at the business school at Big State U. His mom's eyes twinkled every time she told someone about how Sam earned a spot in the B-school as a freshman.

Sam's dad was concerned. "I don't know, son. It sounds like a great opportunity, but dropping out of school? Like I've always said, a college degree is something no one can ever take away from you. And the economy is changing—you saw the tough time Uncle Michael had finding another job after he got laid off last year. Now he's working for half of what he was making before. Without a degree, his 20 years of experience in supply chain management meant next to nothing—all the jobs in his field now require a college degree to even get an interview. You just never know what could happen . . . Can you really trust this Ken guy?"

"He comes from a wealthy, successful family, Dad. And I'll get to learn so much from him—like he said, the kind of stuff I can't learn from a textbook. I want to get in there and just do it. I can go back to school in a few years to finish up. It won't be a big deal. Ken said that's what he did—and look how successful he is now."

Sam's parents gave their blessing reluctantly if he promised to finish out the spring semester. Sam arrived in Houston the third week of May. He'd spent the last month pulling all-nighters developing the Drive U marketing strategy—and trying to fit in time to study for five final exams. Ken never offered to pay him for any of that work, but he was nonetheless excited for the presentation he would be giving to the Houston staff his first week with Drive U. Ken said it would be good for Sam to present the growth strategy since he was the one who had pulled it all together.

The Heights location had two supervisors, Erin and Jake, and a staff of six drivers who taught classes and gave behind-the-wheel training. Sam was excited to meet Erin and Jake. Unfortunately, they were in another meeting all morning and walked into Sam's strategy presentation just as Ken was introducing him.

"Good afternoon, everyone. As you may have heard, we have big plans for the Houston area—and the entire state of Texas! Our new intern, Sam, is here to walk you through those plans. I'm really excited to have Sam joining the team today. In addition to helping me with strategy, Sam will be managing the Heights location. He comes to us from the Business School at Big State U. He's a real go-getter and I know you'll be excited to hear what he has in store for you."

Sam walked up to the front of the room and began his presentation. He thought Erin looked unimpressed and Jake just looked irritated, but Sam carried on since Ken was grinning and nodding as he jotted notes from the back of the room. The drivers seemed anxious and distracted, constantly checking the clock behind Sam. He knew they had a full slate of classes today, but he thought they should be more interested in the company's growth strategy. No one asked any questions after his presentation, so Ken thanked Sam, and everyone clapped and then left the room.

Later that day, Sam was able to catch Jake to introduce himself. He figured that as the most tenured driving instructor—6 years with Drive U—Jake would have some helpful insights into how to help the company "drive into the future" as Ken always said.

"Yeah, hi, Sam. Nice presentation this morning. Looks like you are Ken's new go-to guy," Jake said.

Sam thought he detected some sarcasm in Jake's voice, but he didn't want to jump to any conclusions. "Yeah, I'm really excited about the opportunity to work with you all."

"Yeah, you've got a lot to learn. It's crazy around here. I tried to offer Ken some ideas for making this place run better last year, but he didn't want to hear it."

Sam was a little taken aback to hear Jake talk that way about the company owner, but he also remembered that Ken warned him that Jake was "a complainer who didn't like to work too hard." The next 6 months were a whirlwind. On top of everything else, Ken asked Sam to work with a vendor he hired to create a new scheduling app so customers could schedule their own classes online. It was a lot of detailed negotiation to get the functionality working. Ken didn't understand much about the technology, so Sam had to ask Erin and Jake for input and then relayed the details to the vendor. Sam squeezed in a bit of market research while working on the app, scheduling driving classes, and supervising the staff. Sam was getting overwhelmed and frustrated.

Then, Ken moved Sam from the company's headquarters in the Heights neighborhood to the Memorial neighborhood location, which removed Sam from daily interaction with the rest of the leadership team. As part of his growth-through-acquisition strategy, Ken bought the Memorial location about a year ago. The previous owner treated his employees "like family," so the Memorial staff was not happy about the merger or the change in leadership style. And Ken never spent any time at Memorial, which only amplified the staff's continued longing for "the way things used to be." Ken had first sent Erin to "fix the Memorial problem," but Erin complained the staff there were "just resistant to change" and threatened to quit if Ken didn't bring her back to the Heights.

"I just need you at Memorial for a short time, Sam. Just to clean things up and improve morale, whip them into shape, you know. You're the right guy for the job. That location needs your energy and fresh ideas. Those people are so resistant to any type of change. And you know Erin; she's as lazy as they come. You're the only one I can count on. I just need you there for a short time," Ken reiterated.

Sam agreed, but he didn't feel like he had much of a choice. He thought a short time didn't sound too bad, maybe a month or two. Over time, though, he started working 12- to 14-hour days, 6 days a week with no end in sight. And as a salaried employee, working more hours meant he ended up making less per hour, much less in fact. He hadn't been able to drive home to San Antonio for Thanksgiving either, since Ken insisted that all locations be open on Thanksgiving morning and the day after Thanksgiving. He also missed his grandmother's 80th birthday party. He knew she was disappointed by his absence.

While he'd never been able to find any formal company vacation policies documented, Erin had forewarned Sam that no one was allowed to take time off between May and August because that was Drive U's busiest time of the year. Erin also explained that Sam was essentially going to "lose" a full week's vacation he'd earned because in addition to blocking the summer months off, Ken also didn't allow employees' unused vacation time to "roll over" for potential use in the next year. That meant any earned vacation time Sam wasn't able to actually use by the end of the year was voided.

Sam appreciated the heads-up from Erin—they had developed a good working relationship after working through her initial resistance to "some intern" telling her what to do. He had come to understand her rightful frustration with the lack of operational processes and earned her respect by implementing some of her ideas. Sam had quickly figured out that if he presented Erin's ideas to Ken as his rather than Erin's, Ken was more likely to support them. However, he couldn't shake the feeling that doing this was wrong.

Now, he'd been at Memorial for almost 8 months, and Ken said he'd need him there for several more.

"Like I said, buddy, just a short period of time. I've got a meeting with potential buyers coming up soon. We just need to get the new app launched and open our third location in River Oaks and then I'll have a better feel for what the opportunities might be for you after I sell."

Wait, Sam thought, "*After you sell? . . . Opportunities that might be available? . . .*" Sam was beginning to question Ken's smooth talking.

Sam needed to vent. He called his best friend Connor, who had also left school to work at Drive U.

"I don't know how much longer I can keep this up. And Ken mentioned yesterday he's likely selling the company to investors. I hardly get to do any of the strategic planning anymore, and the app development vendor said Ken hasn't been paying them. That's not how I'd run my business. Now I wonder if he has any intention of promoting me like he promised."

After more venting, Sam and Connor laughed about how college classes and even the challenge of studying for those monster B-school final exams sounded pretty good right about now.

"Can you believe it?" Sam chuckled.

Talking things through with Connor solidified his decision: Sam was going to quit. But he knew he wouldn't be able to go back to Big State U to finish his degree, at least not right away. He'd ruined his GPA that last semester with all the hours he spent working on Drive U's market development strategy. He remembered what his dad had told him about the value of a college degree, and his mom's frequent reminders to be prepared for the unexpected. "Now I know what they meant," he thought to himself.

Sam drove to the Heights location Monday morning. He wanted to pay Ken the respect of telling him in person that he would be quitting in early December to spend the holidays in San Antonio with his parents and register for spring classes at the community college. He hoped Ken wouldn't be too disappointed. He was stunned by Ken's response.

"I understand, Sam. It's a tough business and it's not for everyone. Thanks for letting me know. I'll give the B-school a call tomorrow to see who I can get in here for next semester. There's usually a bunch of kids ready to do the work and rise to the top with an opportunity like this. Best of luck to you back at school."

DISCUSSION QUESTIONS

1. What messages/lessons did Sam learn about college, work, and career from his parents?
2. How did Ken Tomlinson's charismatic leadership influence Sam's anticipatory organizational socialization?
3. When did Sam experience sense giving and who/what influenced Sam's behavior throughout his experience?
4. Name and describe the different transitions Sam experienced throughout his time with Drive U. What role did communication play in these transitions?
5. What ethical issues do you see related to Ken Tomlinson's efforts to persuade undergraduates like Sam to leave college for a job opportunity without first completing their college degrees?

SUGGESTED READINGS

Barnett, K. (2012). Student interns' socially constructed work realities: Narrowing the work expectation-reality gap. *Business Communication Quarterly*, *75*, 271–290. doi:10.1177/1080569912441360

Carr, A. (2000). Critical theory and the management of change in organizations. *Journal of Organizational Change Management*, *13*, 208–220. doi:10.1108/09534810010330869

Dailey, S. L. (2016). What happens before full-time employment? Internships as a mechanism of anticipatory socialization. *Western Journal of Communication*, *80*, 453–480. https://doi.org/10.1080/10570314.2016.1159727

Davis, C. W., & Myers, K. K. (2012). Communication and member disengagement in planned organizational exit. *Western Journal of Communication*, *76*, 194–216. https://doi.org/10.1080/10570314.2011.651250

Jablin, F. M., & Kramer, M. W. (1998). Communication-related sense-making and adjustment during job transfers. *Management Communication Quarterly*, *12*, 155–182. doi:10.1177/0893318998122001

Klatzke, S. R. (2016). I quit! The process of announcing voluntary organizational exit. *Qualitative Research Reports in Communication*, *17*, 44–51. doi:https://doi.org/10.1080/17459435.2015.1088894

Kramer, M. W. (1993). Communication and uncertainty reduction during job transfers: Leaving and joining processes. *Communication Monographs*, *60*, 178–198. doi:10.1080/03637759309376307

Kramer, M. W. (2010). *Organizational socialization: Joining and leaving organizations*. Malden, MA: Polity Press.

Pastorek, A. E. (2015). *Organizational exit dynamics in times of turbulence: Let me tell you the story of how my high hopes were let down* (Unpublished doctoral dissertation). The University of Texas, Austin, Texas.

ONE ORGANIZATION, TWO DIVERGENT EXPERIENCES

A TALE OF TWO PART-TIME EMPLOYEES' ORGANIZATIONAL ASSIMILATION

Michael Sollitto, PhD
Texas A&M University, Corpus Christi

Dansby's Anticipation

"I am really excited to get started at Hershiser's today. I think it will be good to gain some work experience, make some money, and learn to balance my time between work and school. I hope that everything goes alright, though," Dansby told his mother as he completed a brief phone conversation with her while walking from his campus housing to his car.

"I am too, Dansby. You will do fine at Hershiser's," his mother replied. As a 20-year-old college student, Dansby anticipated embarking on a new endeavor, a part-time job that his parents were thrilled about because Dansby's income would assist them in paying his tuition and hopefully provide him some valuable work experience for an enriching career once he completed his finance degree at the university. However, as with any new situation that Dansby encountered, he felt uncertain about how his role at Hershiser's would unfold, the kinds of people that he would meet and work with, and how to be a

This chapter is based on published work: Sollitto, M., Martin, M. M., Dusic, S., Gibbons, K. E., & Wagenhouser, A. (2016). Assessing the supervisor/subordinate relationship involving part-time employees. *International Journal of Business Communication, 53,* 74–96. doi:10.1177/2329488414525462 good employee. "*She's right; things will work out fine for me,*" Dansby uttered to himself as he made his journey to Hershiser's for his first day of work.

Erick's Anticipation

"Ah man, I've got to go to work today," said Erick to his roommate. "It should be a decent gig, help me make some money, but man, we'll just see. I wish I could just stay home and relax," he added as he dragged himself off the couch and walked out the front door to his car. As a 21-year-old college student, Erick dreaded beginning his new job at Hershiser's that day. He departed his last job at a local restaurant because he lost interest in it and never saw much point to his working there.

"We really need you to do well at this job, Erick," Erick's dad said to him over the phone during Erick's commute to Hershiser's.

"I know, Dad. Hopefully it will work out for me."

His parents desperately wanted him to find and keep a job because they wanted him to be successful once he finished his marketing degree, but thus far, he had yet to experience much motivation or success in his part-time job endeavors. "*Maybe this job will be easy, and I can just do a little bit of work and still bring home a decent check,*" Erick uttered to himself after finishing his conversation.

Dansby and Erick Meet Brian and Learn Their Roles

Hershiser's was a small family-owned retail clothing establishment located in the Pleasant Oaks Shopping Mall near where both Dansby and Erick attended college. Hershiser's specialized in men's and women's casual and professional apparel, emphasizing stylish clothes at affordable prices. Brian, an experienced and affable veteran of the retail clothing industry, served as the store manager of Hershiser's. Since becoming store manager of Hershiser's 5 years prior, Brian deftly achieved consistently high sales performance for his store, ranking among the top five performers among all 20 Hershiser's locations each year. Aware of his own pleasant nature, ability to guide and direct his employees, and attain high sales goals, Brian exuded comfort and confidence about his ability to work with employees and lead them toward better performance than they thought possible. He knew how to manage a store, and he liked to develop friendly rapport with all 20 (6 full-time and 14 part-time) of his employees to ascertain their strengths and place them in the best situations to succeed as Hershiser's employees. Brian considered his personal style of managing effective because of the diverse array of employees he tended to manage, especially while working with college-age employees.

At 4:00 p.m. Dansby and Erick arrived at Brian's office located adjacent to the Hershiser's sales floor. "Nice to see you again, Dansby. How have you been doing?" Brian asked as he extended his hand to greet Dansby.

"I'm great, sir. Eager to get started."

"How are you, Erick?" Brian asked as he turned his attention and stretched his hand to Erick.

Erick replied in a lethargic manner, "I'm fine."

Puzzled by Erick's listless demeanor, Brian continued with his preview of Dansby and Erick's training session. "Well then, let's get started. Today we will spend most of our time providing basic information about what we do here at Hershiser's and what your individual responsibilities are as sales associates. I find it useful to sit down in our training room to discuss the basic things like company and store policies. Then we will move to the sales floor to show you the cash registers and teach you how to present yourself to customers." While Brian explained his approach for training, Dansby felt his uncertainty begin to dissipate because Brian made a favorable impression and because Brian seemed to concern himself with essential and useful details. Erick, on the other hand, just wished that Brian would finish, so that he could finish his shift and go home.

After spending time discussing the basic details about being a Hershiser's employee, Brian led Erick and Dansby to the sales floor and spent the next 2 hours introducing them to their coworkers, training them on the cash register, and demonstrating to them the "Hershiser's Way" for folding and presenting merchandise on the sales floor. It was a whirlwind 3 hours of information, demonstration, and practice for his newcomers, so Brian decided to give them a break to let all the information sink in and relax for a little while. Dansby, thankful for the break, tried to mentally organize all the information he had learned in the previous few hours while also contemplating Erick's behavior. Throughout the entire time he had been at work that day, he had been curious about Erick. Erick seemed disinterested and unconcerned with the information Brian shared. Dansby reasoned that this break would be a useful opportunity to acquaint himself with Erick. He knew that they attended the same university, but that was all that Dansby knew about Erick.

"How is the training going for you, Erick?" Dansby asked as they approached the mall food court.

"Eh. Pretty good, I guess. None of that stuff is really all that interesting to me."

"It is a lot of stuff to remember," replied Dansby, hoping to find some common ground about Hershiser's with Erick.

"Yeah," said Erick as he continued walking, clearly disinterested in Dansby's conversation. Interpreting Erick's reluctance to chat anymore, Dansby decided to drop the subject and enjoy his break before returning to training. With the break finished, Dansby and Erick returned to the sales floor to refresh themselves on information that they learned earlier, and listen to Brian as he discussed various scenarios and facilitated practice with cash register transactions to reinforce information he provided throughout the evening.

At 10:00 p.m., the store closing time, Brian patted both of his workers on the back and said, "Nice work, fellas. Good job tonight." Now admittedly, Brian confidently determined that Dansby was truly interested in being a productive sales associate at Hershiser's, but he was unsure about Erick. When the store closed that night and Dansby walked to his car, he felt simultaneously energized because of his new job but also tired from all the information he had encountered. Erick, conversely, walked to his car thinking that this would be just another dull, unexciting job for him.

As the weeks progressed, Dansby felt increasingly comfortable as a member of Hershiser's. However, he did experience a minor conflict with one of his coworkers when he took credit for a substantial purchase, despite his coworker being the one who primarily helped and assisted the customer. Brian, upon learning about the conflict, summoned Dansby to his office and told him that he needed to be extra careful to avoid taking credit for items that other workers had helped customers find and make decisions about. A remorseful Dansby apologized to his coworker and vowed to be smarter about completing transactions with customers who had been assisted by other Hershiser's workers. Despite the conflict, Dansby perceived the situation as a learning experience, and he discovered that he liked working with his coworkers, as he developed friendly relations with all of the other members of Hershiser's. He saw overlap in his work at Hershiser's and the content he was learning in his classes at the local university. He also felt a certain kinship between himself and Hershiser's because he would proudly tell people that he was a sales associate there, and that they should come visit the store sometime. He also knew exactly what he needed to do each day when he entered the store to begin his work shift, and he earned frequent praise from Brian for his sales performance and his general affability on the job.

Because of his performance and Brian's compliments, Dansby no longer felt like a novice in his work role or uncertain about his performance. Most of all, however, Dansby felt a sense of connection with Brian. Dansby could ask Brian for help without feeling like he should already know the answer or that Brian would punish him for asking. He could also negotiate his schedule with Brian, especially whenever Dansby had a big assignment or test approaching in his classes. One thing that Dansby still had difficulty figuring out, however, was Erick. Whenever he worked with Erick or conversed with him, their conversations were stilted and uncomfortable. He also never perceived Erick as enjoying his work at Hershiser's at all. In fact, Erick's apathy toward his work was visible with how frequently he would allow customers to enter and peruse the store without greeting or assisting them, a major violation of Hershiser's organizational values.

One day when Dansby and Erick shared a shift together, Dansby asked Erick how things were going. "Decent. I'm not really excited about being here."

"Why is that?" Dansby followed up.

"Because this is just a silly clothing store. There's no real challenge to it. Plus, Brian has never really treated me all that well; I'm getting fewer hours each week, and I'm tired of it. Brian seems to like you a lot though."

Dansby was unsure what that last statement from Erick truly meant, but Dansby could also ascertain why Brian may have never really treated Erick as favorably as Brian had treated him because Erick never really showed much interest in being a good sales associate. In Dansby's experience, Brian was a fair and considerate manager to everyone at Hershiser's. However, Dansby kept those thoughts to himself and said, "I like it here. I see it as a cool place to work and to develop my skills."

"That's fine for you, but I am probably going to quit, honestly. I see no point in me sticking around here much longer."

"You should give it more time. Maybe it will get better for you," Dansby replied, searching for a nice and supportive thing to say to reduce the awkwardness of their conversation.

"Nah, I think I will turn in my notice tonight."

"Well, I guess you know what is best for your own situation," Dansby said as he saw a customer walking into the store, which thankfully gave him an opportunity to end their conversation to approach the customer. As it turned out, that was the last time that Dansby worked a shift with Erick. Erick put in his two-week notice that night and worked sparingly until his last day as a sales associate for Hershiser's.

Dansby's New Opportunity

"Hey, Dansby!" Brian exclaimed as Dansby walked through the Hershiser's entrance to begin his work shift a few weeks later. "Come chat with me quickly in my office."

Feeling a momentary sense of panic, Dansby tried to remember the previous shifts he had worked to determine if he had done anything wrong. He decided that Brian just wanted to talk with him about something, so he replied, "Sure, Brian. I will be right there." Once Dansby gathered himself, he walked into Brian's office and sat down at the chair across from Brian's desk.

Turning from his computer to face Dansby, Brian began, "Dansby, you've been here a couple of months now. You have been doing some really good work. The customers like you, your coworkers like you, you have grasped the 'Hershiser's Way' extremely well." Brian paused, almost to create even more suspense, Dansby thought to himself. "We are expanding this Hershiser's location because our sales have been so good, so I'll need to hire a few more part-time workers. Given how good you are at working here and handling responsibility, I would like for you to be an assistant manager for us here at Hershiser's. How would you like to be my guy?"

Dansby thought for a few seconds, and then he said, "I would love that opportunity. I'll do it."

DISCUSSION QUESTIONS

1. Considering the five primary information sources that influence occupation choices during anticipatory role socialization, describe how Dansby's experience at Hershiser's will assist him with his career aspirations.

2. Using Uncertainty Management Theory, describe the kinds of uncertainty Dansby experienced as he encountered his new role at Hershiser's, and explain how he managed his uncertainty about his role, including relationships to supervisors and peers.

3. Describe which of the socialization strategies that Brian used to socialize Dansby and Erick.

4. Considering that organizational identification is an important outcome of socialization, compare Dansby and Erick's levels of organizational identification about Hershiser's.

5. Given that Brian prides himself on understanding each of his employees' strengths and weaknesses, explain whether he should have made greater strides to ensure that Erick achieved success at Hershiser's.

SUGGESTED READINGS

Day, D. V., & Miscenko, D. (2016). Leader-member exchange (LMX): Construct evolution, contributions, and future prospects for advancing leadership theory. In. T. N. Bauer & B. Erdogen (Eds.), *The Oxford handbook of leader-member exchange* (pp. 9–22). New York, NY: Oxford.

Gailliard, B. M., Myers, K. K., & Seibold, D. R. (2010). Organizational assimilation: A multidimensional reconceptualization and measure. *Management Communication Quarterly, 24*, 552–578. doi:10.1177/0893318910374933

Kramer, M. W. (2004). *Managing uncertainty in organizational communication.* Mahwah, NJ: Lawrence Erlbaum.

Kramer, M. W., Meisenbach, R. J., & Hansen, G. J. (2013). Communication, uncertainty, and volunteer membership. *Journal of Applied Communication Research, 41*, 18–39. doi:10.1080/00909882.2012.750002

Nonis, S. A., & Hudson, G. I. (2006). Academic performance of college students: Influence of time spent studying and working. *Journal of Education for Business, 81*, 151–179. doi:10.3200/JOEB.81.3.151-159

ETHICS AND DISCLOSURE OF ILLNESS IN THE HIRING PROCESS

8

Jeremy P. Fyke, PhD
Belmont University

"Help Brian Fight Cancer!" The title of the newly set-up GoFundMe page that Bree spent the evening creating said it all. Bree took it live, made a donation, emailed the link to a handful of close relatives, and posted a link on Facebook. Her plea was clear and brief: "Friends, do what you can—share, donate, and, most importantly, pray for Brian's healing, peace, and comfort during this unimaginable time." Then, within minutes of sitting down with her husband to binge-watch *The Fall* on Netflix, Bree got a text, short and sweet— "*Sissy, please take that down. Brian has a job interview next week and doesn't want his diagnosis to bias their hiring process.*"

Just 2 short weeks prior, Brian, 41-year-old father of three, received the worst news anyone can imagine—he had been diagnosed with late-stage colon cancer. He had many tests yet to be run, but early indications were that his condition was dire, with either the possibility of months to live if the cancer was aggressive, and up to 1 year if it was less advanced.

For more than 20 years Brian has enjoyed a successful career in video and audio editing for television and radio, along with freelance volunteer and paid video and audio editing for friends, family, and businesses. He used his skills to help others quite often; his family and friends have

---

This chapter is based on personal experiences.

long been gifted his video editing skills as a wedding present. Full-time, Brian has worked his lifelong passion at various stations throughout their town and region. He has been with his current employer, a prominent local TV station, News6, for nearly 10 years. Even though he was mostly happy where he was, he always kept his "feelers out" for new opportunities, and often went through various rounds of interviews. He remembered something a work mentor told him early in his career, "The best time to leave a job is when you're happy, not when you're miserable." It took him a while to understand that bit of advice, but he had come to appreciate it over the years.

No opportunity had stuck recently, either because it wasn't right for him or he didn't get the offer. They didn't talk about it too much, but Brian's near-constant looking and "job shopping" puzzled Jenny because she saw herself as a "lifer" in her current role as a veterinarian. For Brian, the job at TV5 seemed like such a perfect opportunity. He would be able to continue his current work—primarily video editing—but also be able to do some work on the side for their sibling radio station, WBEL. The cancer diagnosis was flat-out bad timing, as the ad for the job hit his inbox 2 weeks prior. Brian and his wife, Jenny, had much to discuss.

Late on an otherwise normal Tuesday night, a few hours following dinner, after their three kids, Paige, 14, Ryan, 11, and Hank, 7, went to bed, Brian and Jenny sat down on the couch. Their four-bedroom, two-and-a-half bath Midwestern home was modest, but it was all they needed. It felt small at times, but mostly, it was cozy. Lately, it began to seem like a real luxury, along with everything else in their lives.

They knew the conversation needed to happen, but it was hard to get started. Jenny just jumped right in, "Brian, you have to tell them. And I mean *first*, before you even go into the interview. I don't see any way around it."

"How do I even do that?" Brian responded quickly. "I mean, what does that email sound like? 'Hey, I know I applied for this job, but something to think about—I have cancer.'"

Brian is a funny guy, more than capable of sarcasm to match his dry sense of humor, but this was different. Jenny read this response as a symptom of his confusion and frustration.

"Or," Brian continued, "Am I supposed to ask for a face-to-face meeting to talk about this before I even get the interview? That doesn't really follow any protocol and just doesn't seem practical. They'll either think something is up, I'm really impatient, or that I'm a wacko."

Jenny jumped in, "Yeah, I get what you're saying. And I don't know *how* you're supposed to do it, but let's talk about *why*, from their perspective."

"Hold on," Brian insisted. "In the actual interview, they can't ask about health or family-related things, so shouldn't that mean that I also don't have to disclose?"

"I guess," Jenny agreed, hesitantly.

Brian continued, "Or should a woman who's newly pregnant disclose that? They can't ask about it. Isn't all of that about getting a fair shake?"

"I see where you're going with this, yes," Jenny acknowledged and continued, "I know companies can't ask you health-related questions, unless it's pertinent to the job, but I guess I just didn't really think about it going the other way in terms of what you should or shouldn't disclose on the front end."

"Right! And I'm sure most people don't think about that," Brian added confidently.

"Hold on." Jenny begged. "Let's just think about it from their perspective—ethically, practically, economically—whatever. At the end of the day, wouldn't there be a big shock to the employer once you start, and then be a feeling of letdown and dishonesty?"

Brian jumped right back in, "Well, ethically speaking, isn't ethics about fairness? Or equality? Or at least that's part of it, right? Doesn't everyone deserve a fair shot? Isn't that the whole point of EEO, Equal Employment Opportunity, or whatever it's called, protection around different types of questions?"

"Yes, it's exactly about fairness. And what if you started a job and it was totally different than what you expected, roles are different, a boss was totally different, and so on, in a bad way? Is that fair? Think about that side of it," said Jenny.

"Okay," Brian somewhat agreed. "But I'm a fighter, and I want to be able to beat this thing. Shouldn't I get that chance, and, in the process, be able to pursue a job that I think will be a good job fit for me and a good move for us as a family? Maybe the station would see my determination to fight as a good quality? Why does the surprise have to be bad?"

"I guess so. Those are good points," Jenny responded, as she shrugged her shoulders. "But it still just doesn't feel right. And your point about your determination to fight, couldn't that also be an argument to tell them?"

"What do you mean?" Brian asked.

"Well," Jenny continued, "If you *do* tell them you have this, which, for the record, I still think is the right thing to do anyway, and let them know you're going to fight your butt of to beat it, they might admire that grit and determination."

Brian nodded his head for a moment and, despite making some good points and feeling good about them, was still clearly ambivalent. Letting out a quiet, sarcastic laugh that seemed to say, "*This is just so ridiculous.*" He continued, "You're right. The ironic thing in all of this is that I would want to know if I were doing the hiring. It would be a big shock. If I hired someone and then found something like this out, I would be pissed and feel betrayed. I would feel like it's a waste of time—mine as the interviewer and ours as a company. But I still want this to play out."

Jenny jumped back in, "Let what play out—the first round, second round, all the way to getting the offer? Then you'll tell them? After you get the offer?"

"I don't know," Brian said. "But let's consider the possibility that I recover completely and then this is moot. What good have I done to sound the alarm for nothing? If I tell them now, and I don't get the opportunity, then I would regret it forever."

Jenny, getting frustrated, remarked, "'Forever?' The other part of this is—why can't you just be happy with your job? I remember when we were in school we learned a lot about job interviews, but I didn't see us—you—continuing to apply and interview all the time like you seem to do."

"Hold on. We're getting off topic here, aren't we?" Brian replied.

"Not really," Jenny said. "This is an important issue that we should talk about because maybe this whole thing would be irrelevant if you weren't so restless in your work."

"Okay," Brian conceded, and indicated that he would at least have the conversation. "I just don't see my work as this job or that job; it's a lifelong process where I'm always looking around, keeping my eyes and ears open. To be honest, I also just like the process of looking and interviewing."

Jenny replied, "But you've got a good job, and it's secure. Interviewing is a hassle, putting yourself out there like that time and again."

Brian interrupted, "I just don't look at it like that. I see the process, and especially the interviews, as a way to learn from people and make connections. If I don't get it, I sit back and ask myself *why*, what am I missing, and figure out what I need to add to my tool bag to set myself apart or do my job better."

Leaning her head to the left in thought, Jenny replied, "Yeah, but the other thing to think about, or at least that I think about a lot is that your profession, especially in our town, is a pretty small family. Won't word get around that you never seem content and are always job shopping?"

"Eh, maybe," Brian shrugged and lifted his palms upward. "Or, they might see it as a guy who constantly wants to learn and make connections."

Jenny smirked as if to almost acknowledge the work Brian was doing at rationalizing his job-shopping prowess. "Okay, okay. I can see you think this is a positive thing, this job hunting. What about another angle to this that I think is important?"

"Go on," Brian encouraged.

"How long have you been at News6? 10 years? What about the relationships you've built? Won't you need those to help get you through this fight? You've got some close friends there that you can trust and lean on for support in the coming months. If you go to TV5, you're starting over."

Brian nodded his head slowly, as if to indicate that he agreed but had not thought of it that way. "Yep, that's true. I mean, I know some of those guys from different events I've been to, but definitely nothing like the relationships I have here. I also hadn't really fully thought of what's ahead and that the people I work with might be helpful in that way."

"Or," Jenny continued, "That they might be more understanding when you're asking for time off if or when chemo starts and you don't feel like going in. Just think about the timing of this—in all likelihood you'd be starting chemo around the time you're starting your new job."

"Yes, and, so?" Brian questioned.

"So?" Jenny replied, "Well, what would those first few weeks look like when you're in orientation and training and whatnot and needing to miss work? I feel like it would not only be hard practically speaking, but also people would start talking. Wouldn't you get off on the wrong foot?"

Brian could see her point, but he still had more questions than answers. "Wrong foot? What does my personal stuff have to do with work? If I'm *working* while at *work*, they shouldn't care, right?"

Jenny replied, "Well, another thing I just thought of, from TV5's perspective is, what if you tell them now and get the job anyway? Aren't they better able to help you get started and can work with you more proactively if you're needing time off?"

Brian gasped as he shook his head and rubbed his forehead, "Whew. We've covered a lot of ground here. Thanks for letting me bounce so many ideas around. To be honest, before we talked, I was 80% sure I didn't want to tell them; I might be around 60% now. I just don't know what to do. All I know is the interview is next week, so I gotta figure this out."

DISCUSSION QUESTIONS

1. Should Brian disclose the cancer diagnosis? Why or why not? If yes, at what point in the process, and how (e.g., email, meeting) should he disclose the diagnosis?
2. How would you view his decision whether to disclose from the various perspectives noted in the case—ethical, practical, economic—from Brian *and* the company's perspective?
3. Brian lists several reasons why he enjoys ongoing job shopping and interviewing. What do you enjoy or not enjoy about the process, and what are the benefits and drawbacks?
4. Should employers be able to ask about health-related issues that have potential long-term implications (e.g., chronic illness, pregnancy)? Why or why not?
5. Brian's initial fear we see in the case study is that the prospective employer would see the GoFundMe page online and that would interfere with the process. What are the benefits and drawbacks of employers using the Web to vet candidates?
6. Would you classify Brian as a segmenter who keeps strict work-life boundaries or integrator who allows the two to overlap? Note instances where you see this revealed in the case, and discuss the benefits and drawbacks to each strategy.

SUGGESTED READINGS

Berkelaar, B. L., & Buzzanell, P. M. (2014). Reconceptualizing fit (assessments) in personnel selection: Employers' sensemaking about cybervetting. *Journal of Applied Communication Research, 42*, 456–476. doi:10.1080/00909882.2014.95459

Peebles, K. A. (2012). Negligent hiring and the information age: How state legislatures can save employers from inevitable liability. *William and Mary Law Review, 35*, 1396–1433. Retrieved from http://scholarship.law.wm.edu/cgi/viewcontent.cgi?article=3427&context=wmlr

Solove, D. J. (2007). *The future of reputation. Gossip, rumor, and privacy on the Internet.* New Haven, CT: Yale University Press.

SOCIALIZING WITH COWORKERS ABOUT WRONGDOING AT THE ANNUAL COMPANY BARBEQUE

Nicole A. Ploeger-Lyons, PhD
University of Wisconsin, La Crosse

Greg Ormes, PhD
University of Wisconsin, La Crosse

Daniel crossed the parking lot with nervous anticipation. He was heading to a local park where his new company, Rogers Corporation, was hosting its annual company barbeque. Daniel had just started working in Human Resources at Rogers the previous Monday, and he was experiencing the stress and uncertainty that come when transitioning into a new position and organization. This barbeque would be his first opportunity to interact with his coworkers outside of the workplace and to meet people from other departments. He was hoping they might provide some support and advice to him as a newcomer. So, while nervous about feeling like the odd person out, Daniel was eager to make new connections and learn about his coworkers and their experiences in the organization.

As he approached the park pavilion, Daniel was relieved to see Kat, one of his Human Resources coworkers with whom he had been training during the past week. Kat was talking with a handful of other employees when she spotted Daniel and waved him over. "Daniel!

This chapter is based on published work: Ploeger, N. A., & Bisel, R. S. (2013). The role of identification in giving sense to unethical organizational behavior: Defending the organization.
Management Communication Quarterly, 27, 155–184. doi:10.1177/0893318912469770

I'm so glad you made it! Have you had the chance to meet any of these folks?" Kat asked.

"No," Daniel replied. "I don't believe I've had the pleasure."

Daniel exchanged handshakes as Kat introduced him to four other Rogers Corporation employees—Anna, Harriett, Stan, and Baker. Daniel learned that these individuals worked in various departments across the organization. Anna had worked in accounting for over a decade. Harriett and Stan were both in sales and had been with Rogers Corporation for 8 years each. Baker was also a seasoned employee, with 18 years of experience in various Rogers Corporation departments and locations. Daniel was relieved to be making some new connections, and the group seemed warm and welcoming to Daniel.

Over the next 30 minutes, the group exchanged life updates and talked about hobbies and shared interests before Daniel took the opportunity to seek some information about work-related questions he encountered during his first week. "Do you all know Elena, my supervisor?"

Everyone in the group nodded, and Kat—being in Human Resources with Daniel—added, "Of course. I've worked with Elena for a long time. She was my first supervisor here, too."

Daniel continued, "On Thursday, I asked her if Fridays were more casual around the office. She laughed and said that she 'always likes to keep it casual.' I'm not sure what to make of that."

This provoked a laugh from everyone in the group and a few murmurs like "that's Elena for you" and "sounds about right." After a moment, Daniel, still feeling confused, asked more directly, "So, do we do casual dress on Fridays or not?"

Kat explained, "Elena can be playful. She is never too strict on dress, but it is important to her that we always look and act professionally. Most people around the office tend to be a bit more casual on Fridays than the rest of the week."

Though fairly mundane, this bit of information helped Daniel feel more secure about the office dress code, and he gained some direction on how to read his new supervisor. When prompted by his new coworkers about what else he had questions about, Daniel decided to continue seeking details on topics of which he was uncertain. "In my previous job, promotions and bonuses were tied really closely with annual reviews."

As Daniel hoped, this prompt opened a dialogue about the process of promotion at Rogers Corporation. Some in the group expressed frustration over the criteria used to reward employees, while others were pleased and thought the system was fair. Through this discussion, Daniel was relieved to learn more about promotions and bonuses. In addition, the group guided him to the specific part of the lengthy organizational handbook where he could find more details. Daniel made a note in his phone to remind himself to look at the handbook on Monday for more information.

After getting the scoop on promotion processes and such, Daniel finally worked up the courage to ask about something that had been a substantial source of concern for him. "So, I've been reading online about the class-action lawsuit at the corporate office. Do any of you know much about it?" Daniel asked. "I heard that there is talk of gender discrimination? What do you all think about these accusations?"

An awkward silence descended upon the group as members shared some knowing glances and difficult-to-read expressions. After a few moments, Kat broke the silence, "I'm not sure if that's something we should be talking about, especially not here."

Collectively, though, they explained to Daniel that most of their knowledge on the situation is vague and uncertain. While they have all heard rumors of gender discrimination, there are no official statements, and most knowledge is based on office chit-chat and unconfirmed reports. They agreed that gender discrimination is unethical, but the whole situation at Rogers Corporation was still quite ambiguous. Kat hoped her coworkers would just leave it at that and move on to a different topic of conversation. Baker, however, seemed to want to continue to discuss the situation. "I heard it's just a rumor, anyhow," Baker interjected. "I know a lot of people up at corporate, and that just doesn't sound like our organization. It's not part of our culture."

Anna nodded and chimed in, "Yeah, I mean, look—I've been working here for 14 years now, and I can tell you that this company takes care of its people. I've *never* felt like I was being treated unfairly because I'm a woman, and whenever I've had some other issue or complaint, I was always listened to and taken seriously. I don't know if something happened at corporate, but I know that I work for a good company."

"That's right," Stan said. "Let's be real here, too, though. It's not like the company is perfect, but is there really such thing as a perfect place to work? Everyone here really does do their best to treat people fairly, and when I hear rumors like this, I like to remind myself that there are always two sides to every story. What matters is that *if* something happened, they get to the bottom of it. I'm sure it's not as big of a thing as it's being made out to be. You know how the rumor mill and media outlets always blow things out of proportion."

Daniel was relieved to be hearing such reassuring things from his coworkers about his new place of work. After all, who wants to be employed at an organization that is currently known for rampant gender discrimination? Daniel's relief was mixed with some worry and hesitation. "*Are they just trying to put a positive spin on the situation to make me feel better about being a new employee? Could there be more to the story?*" he thought to himself. He decided to dig a little deeper. "Do any of you know the people who are involved?" Daniel asked out loud.

Harriett nodded slowly with a look of skepticism. "I've heard rumors," she said, "but it doesn't sound right to me. I've worked with one of the people being accused. He's maybe the least lecherous person I've ever met, and I can't imagine him discriminating against anyone. He was once a great mentor to me, and he always made me feel comfortable at Rogers Corporation. He's fair, honest, and kind. If he's denying it, I believe him."

"That's why I don't think there's anything to this at all," Baker added. "It doesn't add up. It's got to be based on some misunderstanding or rumor."

Kat looked uncomfortable and spoke up again, "I think we should be careful talking about this. Those burgers look done! Let's go eat." Her efforts to redirect the conversation failed.

"He deserves to have his side told, too," Anna noted, ignoring Kat's comments. "He's a good guy. He's been around forever, and I bet many of us wouldn't have jobs if it wasn't for him. This is a company we can be proud of, so I think he and Rogers Corporation deserve the benefit of the doubt. I consider it part of my job to remind people about how good this organization is before we get an undeserved reputation. I am proud to have spent over a decade of my life working here."

"What do you think will happen next?" Daniel asked.

"Nothing," Baker replied quickly. "I have been with Rogers Corporation for 18 years now, and I've seen stuff like this happen before. I'll bet people just forget about all of this within a couple of weeks. You know why? Gender discrimination does not happen here. That's just not us."

"Yeah," Stan added. "Rumors like this get spread, but at the end of the day, this is a better place to work than most. Even if there was some kind of misunderstanding, it will all blow over. Companies just like us deal with this stuff all the time."

"I agree. I'm not going to give it any more thought unless I hear some hard facts that would change my mind," said Harriett. "I'm going to trust what I know, and what I know is that he's a good guy who has always been truthful with me. It's like the old saying goes, 'Don't believe everything you read until all the facts come out.'"

"Okay, okay! Seriously, we should stop now," Kat reiterated. "There's *got* to be something more positive to talk about with our newest coworker! Like those burgers. Let's go get some before they're gone!" she said, smiling toward Daniel. The group laughed and agreed.

After eating, Daniel teamed up with Kat, Anna, Harriett, Stan, Baker, and others to beat last year's defending champions in the annual kickball game. As the day continued, Daniel was pleased to meet many more Rogers employees, and he began to feel welcome and secure in his new job now that he had been able to hang out with his coworkers outside of the office. From the information he gained as well as his interactions and observations at the company event, Daniel felt that he was right to sign his contract with Rogers. He was assured that Rogers truly was a good place to work.

When the barbeque ended, Daniel and Kat walked back to their cars together. Daniel was reflecting positively on the conversations he had shared with the group. From seemingly simple topics like Casual Fridays, to a heavier discussion about the class-action lawsuit, he felt better with the information he had gained. He thanked Kat for being so open with him even though he was "the new guy." He was relieved that they all had such positive things to say about Rogers Corporation and that they largely denied the rumors he had read online. As he approached his car, he admitted to Kat (and to himself), "I had been nervous about what I was getting into if there really was a scandal emerging at Rogers. It's enough stress and uncertainty just being the new employee, much less the new employee at a potentially unethical organization. So, to hear you all defend the organization and dismiss the rumors really puts me at ease. Thanks for being so great, Kat. I really value your thoughts, and hope you might be willing to be a mentor to me." Kat noted how happy she was to have another great colleague in Human Resources and that she would do whatever she could to help Daniel succeed at Rogers.

As Daniel got into his car, Kat found herself wondering whether she should offer any additional information to him. Being in Human Resources, he was bound to discover soon what she already knew for certain—Rogers Corporation *does* discriminate against females in pay and promotions. Legal investigations confirmed it. She has read the legal reports and has heard trusted females' accounts of hitting the "glass ceiling" at Rogers. In fact, she is one of them. While Kat is relieved that a settlement agreement has been reached, and that Rogers is revising harassment policies and reviewing the current pay and promotion practices, she cannot help but come back to what she knows to be true: Yes, Rogers is a great place for many of its employees, but gender discrimination is *unethical* and it *is* happening at Rogers. As Kat closed her car door, she asked herself, "*So why can't I say that to my coworkers and friends? I am certain of what is happening, but I just can't bring myself to say it out loud.*"

DISCUSSION QUESTIONS

1. How do you see Uncertainty Management Theory functioning for Daniel as he attempts to understand his new organization?

2. What role do informal conversations like the ones at the annual company barbeque play in the socialization process of new employees? How might this informal socialization differ from the formal socialization that Daniel likely experienced during his first week at Rogers Corporation?

3. What information-seeking strategies does Daniel use to learn more about his new role and organization?

4. What types of peer social support are being sought by Daniel, and how (if at all) is support being provided by his coworkers?

5. What are the possible implications for how newcomers like Daniel make sense of an organization's culture and ethics when formal and/or informal mentors defend the organization's wrongdoing? What are some of the defensive strategies communicated by Rogers Corporation's veteran employees?

6. Considering that the allegations of gender discrimination at Rogers Corporation are true, how might the kind of talk presented in this case shape employees' willingness to accept that their organization is engaging in unethical behavior? How could employees practice more ethical communication in order to actuate needed change?

SUGGESTED READINGS

Brown, A. D., & Starkey, K. (2000). Organizational identity and learning: A psychody-namic perspective. *Academy of Management Review, 25,* 102–120.

Gioia, D. A., & Chittipeddi, K. (1991). Sensemaking and sensegiving in strategic change initiation. *Strategic Management Journal, 12,* 433–448. doi:10.1002/smj.4250120604

Ploeger, N. A., & Bisel, R. S. (2013). The role of identification in giving sense to unethical organizational behavior: Defending the organization. *Management Communication Quarterly, 27,* 155–184. doi:10.1177/0893318912469770

A CONSULTANT INVESTIGATES TURNOVER AT SMA COMPANIES

Vernon D. Miller, PhD
Michigan State University

Kenneth J. Levine, PhD
Michigan State University

Emma E. Kinney, MA
Michigan State University

A few months ago, representatives from a state's manufacturing association (SMA) sought Peri Barkman's help. Peri had 10 years of experience as an organizational consultant. At a meeting attended by the association's officers and staff, they asked her to conduct research to learn reasons for employees leaving their organizations for other nearby ones. Addressing the causes of voluntary turnover has always been of interest to Peri, so she agreed to the project.

The Project

The SMA was a nonprofit entity that aimed to foster manufacturing in the state by providing networking opportunities, information about policies and benefit packages, and training grants to member organizations. Further, these manufacturing organizations came together to discuss their collective concerns and to advocate for local and regional issues facing their industries. The state government and dues from

---

This case is based on the authors' experiences.

organizational members supported a small, professional staff that follows the directives of elected officers. Peri's primary contacts with the SMA were with the executive director and the association's president.

Manufacturing jobs accounted for 15% of employment in the state, producing high-end furniture, automobile parts and assemblies, lasers, fabricated metal products, medical supplies, and specialty chemicals, among others. As explained at the meeting, the state's economy had recovered from a severe recession, and unemployment levels had dropped to an all-time low. After years of stagnant wages and layoffs, the tide had turned in favor of workers. For example, skilled machinists were in high demand, and they could readily find a new job at a slightly higher pay scale. Better benefit packages, shorter commutes to work, and the appeal of a fresh start were luring valued workers to other companies. How should SMA manufacturing firms face this problem? Some companies were willing to increase their hourly wages and modify their benefit packages, but, they asked, *what insight can she offer into employees' motivations to leave or stay?*

As part of Peri's contract, she agreed to conduct focus group interviews in several organizations that were representative of the SMA worker base. Afterwards, based on information gleaned from these interviews, she planned to collect survey data using a sample of their member organizations and provide a report to the Association on her findings and recommendations.

However, Peri knew that companies throughout the state laid off all but the very best employees during the recession, while requiring these workers to work weekends to maintain their productive schedules, inventories, and competitive edge. Surviving employees were initially grateful for employment and extra income from weekend overtime pay. However, as the months have turned into years, required worker overtime was associated with fatigue and burnout. Television news programs recently ran special reports related to work–family conflicts arising from worker stress.

In preparing for the focus group interviews, she reviewed the research literature and found several established predictors of employees' voluntary turnover: dissatisfaction with pay or benefits, high levels of stress related to work assignments or conditions, and interpersonal difficulties with coworkers or antagonism with their immediate supervisor. These same factors were also associated with a lack of employee commitment to the organization.

Focus Group Interviews

Peri initiated a series of focus groups held at four SMA member organizations. She hoped to gain an understanding of the workings of each organization. The organizations were quite diverse—there were traditional manufacturing companies with mostly high-school-educated workers as well as a high-tech manufacturing firm where the employees held graduate degrees. In each case, the Human Resource

Managers arranged the setting and selected participants for the interviews. Peri had no input into the location of the group sessions or selection of participants. In all, there were a total of 50 employees across four focus groups.

Organization #1 was a family-owned, traditional manufacturing firm, primarily producing parts for the auto industry. The founder's son recently took the reins of leadership, having guided the firm through a downsizing 8 years earlier. Many of the 200 mostly male employees had worked for the firm for over 15 years, and they were a tight-knit group. Few new employees were hired after the downsizing, even though demand for their products had increased to levels higher than before the downsizing. From the start of the focus group, it was apparent that employees were angry. Four exemplary statements from employees with 25+ years of experience at the firm caught Peri's attention:

> Sam complained, "I'm sick of all the 'required overtime.' I had to work almost every weekend and that meant I missed several of my kids' soccer and softball games." He mentioned, "My wife is angry that I'm never around." . . . Of course, I like the money, but I hate the extra work."
>
> William discussed that "The boss will occasionally pop-in on weekends for a short time while he and his buddies have to stay and work."
>
> David admitted, "The only reason I'm still here is the money. I make a good salary. I really liked the old man that founded the company, but the son is a jerk."
>
> When Louis said, "I'd leave right now if the right offer came along," it seemed that everyone in the room nodded their heads in agreement.

Organization #2 was also a traditional manufacturing plant owned by a multinational company that produces replacement parts for the human body, such as hip joints and prosthetics. Peri was surprised when only three employees entered the room for the interview—one employee held a managerial position with 20+ years at the company and two engineering interns from the local university.

Little information of value was forthcoming from this interview. The interns were reluctant to say anything other than they liked their work. The manager talked at length about the firm's various products. However, near the end of the interview, the manager said something shocking, "You know our 250 regular employees? Well, we have 100 'temporary' employees working full-time. Officially, they work for an employment agency. They get the same wages and health care plus vacation benefits as our regular ones. But they are not on our books in case we need to downsize or upsize."

Peri drove off thinking, "*And if there are performance issues, employees know the company has trained replacements in the wings.*"

Organization #3 was a high-tech manufacturing organization producing vaccines and chemical applications. This workforce was highly educated. These focus group participants (averaging 7.5 years employment) generally liked working at this firm. Comments from two participants stood out:

> Wendy said, "Let's face it; this is a male-dominated field and I'm the only woman here." She did not seem to be upset by this; rather it was a matter-of-fact statement. As the only women, she said, "Management has no idea about work-life balance, and there are no family-friendly benefits."
>
> Mike noted, "I like working here," but he said, "the company lacks a strong unifying culture—each department seems to work independently of one-another." He also alluded to a constant turnover of employees in key positions. Mike was annoyed that "The firm had just hired a new HR manager; he has an impossible job as my friends are leaving for jobs that pay more."

Organization #4 was another traditional manufacturing firm that modified steel wires (aka rebar) for other manufacturing firms. The plant was loud and dirty. The participants (all with 12+ years of experience) were very content with the company, and there was little, if any, sense that anyone in the group planned to look for a new position elsewhere.

Peri's notes from the interview state that employees seem to feel the company was fair to them, they liked their coworkers on a personal level, and they did not mind the lack of variation in job duties. She was surprised that the employees specifically mentioned that they wished there was affordable housing near the plant and suggested that this might be a reason to look for a new position. The commute time was an issue for many employees.

In reviewing her notes from all four organizations, Peri added two more observations: (1) Employees consistently expressed great satisfaction with the quality of their work and wanted to do a good job; and (2) employees appreciated their employment but seemed acutely aware that economic volatility will likely lead to another round of layoffs.

The Survey and Its Results

SMA officers and staff insisted that Peri develop a survey that employees could complete in 20 minutes or less. She also agreed to measure commitment to the employer, which she knew was strongly negatively associated with voluntary turnover. The SMA felt that their member organizations would be more likely to participate if Peri asks for employee's report of their "commitment" versus the likelihood that they would "quit."

Information from focus group interviewees, their emotional tone, and the literature review aided Peri developing survey questions on:

(a) supervisor–employee relationship,
(b) coworker relationships,

(c) perceptions of top management,
(d) work and life stressors,
(e) their job satisfaction, and
(f) organizational commitment.

SMA officers and staff identified a sample of representative manufacturing companies. The sample included nine organizations, ranging from 60 to 2,000 employees and represented high- and low-tech manufacturing, a host of manufactured products, and local, national, and international ownership. Peri insisted that employee participation in the survey must be voluntary and no management or supervisory personnel could be present during data collection. If an employee wished not to participate, he or she could return the survey blank or incomplete.

Over the next several months, she collected approximately 850 survey responses, of which over 700 were useable for data analyses. The overall sample was mostly male (75%, female 25%), ranging in age from 18 to 71 with a mean and median of 40. Participants in the overall sample were also evenly distributed in length of employment, representing a range of ethnicities and formal education (25% attended or completed high school, 55% completed college credits or earned a degree, 20% completed graduate credits or finished a graduate degree). Nineteen percent of employees worked at their company for 1 year or less, 32% for 2–5 years, 20% for 6–10 years, 13% for 11–15 years, 8% for 16–20 years, and 8% for 20+ years.

When examining the results (see Table 10.1), Peri thought to herself, "*Hmm. I see that organizational commitment is moderately high. The scores on coworker supportiveness, unit standards, and supervisor supportiveness suggest that the employees feel rather positive about their workgroup. Also, looks like work stress is pretty much a nonfactor.*"

As she continued to review the numbers, she considered, "*On the correlation matrix, which tells me the strength and direction of the relationships between variables, I see that organizational commitment is most closely associated with employee perceptions of top management's openness to feedback, satisfaction with pay, supervisory engagement, and satisfaction with benefits. Coworker supportiveness and perceptions of the work unit having high quality standards tend to go hand-in-hand. Perceptions of top management openness, satisfaction with pay, and satisfaction with benefits have strong positive correlations with each other.*"

The correlations led Peri to think, "*I better run a regression analysis, too, to see if I can predict a linear relationship between one or more independent variables with a dependent variable. A stepwise regression will permit me to enter variables one at a time based on the strength of their association with the dependent variable.*"

Table 10.1. Means[a] and Correlation Matrix[b] (based on valid 730 responses)

	Mean	(1)	(2)	(3)	(4)	(5)	(6)	(7)	(8)
(1) Organizational commitment	3.43	1.00							
(2) Coworker supportiveness	4.00	.33	1.00						
(3) Work unit holding high standards	3.96	.41	.66	1.00					
(4) Top management openness	2.85	.60	.34	.34	1.00				
(5) Satisfaction with pay	2.90	.51	.25	.25	.44	1.00			
(6) Satisfaction with benefits	3.14	.43	.25	.25	.50	.50	1.00		
(7) Work stress	2.54	−.13	−.03	−.03	−.03	−.01	.02	1.00	
(8) Supervisor engagement	3.82	.49	.50	.50	.47	.30	.28	−.12	1.00

[a] Mean (1 low, 5 high).

[b] With $N = 730$, any correlation greater than .10 is significant at $p < .01$.

Peri reviewed the regression table (see Table 10.2) and concluded, "*Well, this is rather obvious—the greatest predictor of employee commitment is employee perceptions of top management's openness to feedback, suggestions, and criticism. Openness alone accounts for 36% of the 52% explanatory information captured by survey data.*"

"*I see that top management openness is the primary predictor of employee commitment in six of the nine organizations, and it's the second most important predictor in another organization. Wow— that means that in seven of nine organizations the perception of top management openness is the most important predictor of employee commitment. This is not what I expected.*"

The story of the data started to become clear: "*So, if the overall mean (M = 2.85/5.00) of top management openness is relatively low, then those who perceive that their top management isn't receptive to feedback or criticism have little commitment to their employer. These folks are likely to quit.*"

Looking at the regression table further, she noticed with relief that satisfaction with pay and the supervisory relationship in this sample remain foundational to retaining employees, which findings are in line with major nationwide studies. In her mind, she concludes, "*The three most important variables in the SMA are top management openness, satisfaction with pay, and supervisory engagement.*"

Table 10.2. Overall Stepwise Regression Analysis Predicting Organizational Commitment

			Model Summary						
					Change Statistics				
Enter	R	R Square	Standardized Beta Coefficient	t	R Square Change	F Change	df1	df2	Sig. F Change
Top management openness	.61	.38	.36	14.31	.38	417.72	1	729	.0001
Satisfaction with pay	.66	.44	.25	10.34	.07	84.29	1	728	.0001
Supervisory engagement	.69	.48	.18	7.83	.04	53.37	1	727	.0001
Work unit standards	.70	.50	.21	5.18	.02	20.08	1	726	.0001
Work stress	.71	.51	.11	5.58	.01	12.79	1	725	.0001
Coworker supportiveness	.72	.51	.11	3.90	.01	10.32	1	724	.001
Satisfaction with benefits	.72	.52	.06	3.25	.003	3.89	1	723	.049

Peri's Dilemma

Peri planned a meeting the next week with Human Resource managers and executives from each of the surveyed organizations. Leaders from other SMA organizations would also attend. She needed to present a report that gave an accurate representation of the analysis and its implications.

The implications of the findings have placed Peri in an awkward position. The SMA hired her to give answers. She believed that "sugarcoating" results or telling her clients what they want to hear instead of what they need to hear was unacceptable. Yet Peri believed there were three unique audiences with possible competing interests.

- *SMA Leadership.* High employee turnover rates were associated with significant costs, which concerned the manufacturing community. SMA member organizations were losing workers in a labor market where quality hires were scarce, resulting in lower member profits. In addition, when SMA firms lose employees to another SMA firm, hostilities could erupt within the association. Based on the findings, how should the SMA work with member organizations to reduce voluntary turnover?

- *HR Managers in the Nine Participating Organizations.* In most cases, she surmised that the HR managers were aware of employee distrust in top management in seven of the nine manufacturing plants. How can she tell HR managers to implicate their bosses as a key source of turnover? HR managers also like to be employed.
- *CEOs.* It's true that voluntary turnover was eroding each firm's overall profitability, but each organization was making money despite turnover. What do CEOs have to gain by trying to appear to be more open? Why should they pay attention to Peri's findings when the companies were profitable? How does she present the findings without placing the CEOs on the defensive?

Peri must take care to craft messages that will speak not only to her goals and interests, but to the goals and interests of the diverse SMA audiences.

DISCUSSION QUESTIONS

1. What would be Frederick Taylor's advice to top management based on his theory and the study's findings?
2. What would be Elton Mayo and Douglas McGregor's advice to top management based on their theories and the study's findings?
3. What are some factors that lead to line workers' concerns that their feedback might not reach top management? What are factors that interfere with top management's messages not reaching line workers?
4. What reasons do employees provide for voluntarily exiting their workplaces in the focus groups and survey? In what ways are these reasons different and similar?
5. What influence can one employee's voluntary exit have on others who remain?

SUGGESTED READINGS

Feeley, T. H., Moon, S. I., Kozey, R. S., & Slowe, A. S. (2010). An erosion model of employee turnover based on network centrality. *Journal of Applied Communication Research, 38*, 167–188. doi.org/10.1080/00909881003639544

Mease, J. J. (2016). Embracing discursive paradox: Consultants navigating the constitutive tensions of diversity work. *Management Communication Quarterly, 30*, 59–83. doi.org/10.1177/0893318915604239

Miller, V. D., Johnson, J. R., & Grau, J. (1994). Antecedents to willingness to participate in a planned organizational change. *Journal of Applied Communication Research, 22*, 59–80. doi.org/10.1080/00909889409365387

Montgomery, D. J., Heald, G. R., MacNamara, S. R., & Pincus, L. B. (1995). Malpractice and the communication consultant: A proactive approach. *Management Communication Quarterly, 8*, 368–384. doi.org/10.1177/0893318995008003005

Plax, T. G. (1991). Understanding applied communication inquiry: Researcher as organizational consultant. *Journal of Applied Communication Research, 19,* 55–70. doi.org/10.1080/00909889109365292

Susskind, A. M. (2007). Downsizing survivors' communication networks and reactions: A longitudinal examination of information flow and turnover intentions. *Communication Research, 34,* 156–184. doi.org/10.1177/0093650206298068

BIG SHOES TO FILL

ORGANIZATIONAL CULTURE, MENTORSHIP, AND NETWORKS DURING CAREER CHANGE

Sean M. Eddington, MS
Purdue University

Jessica A. Pauly, PhD
Utah Valley University

"SURPRISE!" the crowd exclaimed as Dr. Gloria F. Bartlett entered the wine bar on a balmy summer night. In shock, Gloria looked back at Lou, the community engagement director for the Bethenny Jones Consulting Group (Jones Consulting), who had coordinated getting her to the event on time.

"You knew this was happening and didn't tell me! Is this why you kept asking me questions to stall me?" Gloria said in an accusatory tone.

Lou's cheeks reddened, "Busted!"

Gloria and Lou walked further into the wine bar, where Gloria was met with hugs from Shannon, her research director, and Veronica, the program coordinator. Together, Gloria, Lou, Shannon, and Veronica comprise the four-person team that oversaw the day-to-day functioning of Jones Consulting. On this special evening, Veronica, Lou, and Shannon were hosting a surprise going-away party for their director, Dr. Gloria Bartlett, who had recently announced that she was leaving Jones Consulting. After 3 years serving as director (and nearly two decades working with Jones Consulting), Bartlett was going to be missed by many.

The presented case is based on personal experience.

Jones Consulting was a nonprofit consulting group started by Bethenny Jones, a glass ceiling–shattering partner and the first female CEO of Franciscan Consulting Group (Franciscan). After she retired, Jones served on the Franciscan Consulting Group's Board of Directors and donated $5.75 million to create a separate wing of the consulting group—Jones Consulting. The mission of Jones Consulting was to enhance leadership opportunities for women in the technology industry through research, community engagement, and collaboration.

As Gloria walked into the party, she was stunned by the number of people who had shown up to surprise her—a diverse group of people (colleagues from the Franciscan Consulting Group, colleagues from professional organizations, community activists from across the metropolitan area, and her family). After a quick round of hugs from her team, Gloria grabbed a plate of food and a glass of red wine as party attendees flocked to her. The rest of the Jones Consulting team gathered near the wine bar's stage.

"That was so good! She was shocked!" Shannon exclaimed. "What else do we need to do, Veronica?"

"I think we're good. We'll give her a few minutes to mingle, and then we'll start the program. The microphones are set up, and I bet everyone is excited to toast Gloria," Veronica stated. "Let's get the program started in a few minutes."

The team nodded, began gathering their parting gifts for Gloria, and went to the stage of the wine bar. Veronica tapped on the microphone, and the roar of conversations within the venue slowed. Unaware of what was going on, Gloria faced the stage as she took small bites of her macaron.

"Good evening, everyone! I'm Veronica. For the last 3 years, I have had the pleasure, honor, and privilege to work for and with Gloria as Jones Consulting's program coordinator. The emails you've received asking for awards nominations, attending our programs—they came from me. We are here to honor, celebrate, and thank Gloria not only for her work at Jones Consulting, but also for her advocacy, her mentorship, and her commitment to making a positive impact in the technology industry. When Gloria first announced she was leaving, I think I speak for many when I say, we were a little gobsmacked. We were heartbroken . . . " Veronica's voice began to crack, and her eyes started to well up with tears.

Two Months Prior

Gloria returned to her office after a holiday break with news. For months, Gloria had quietly been searching for a new role. The truth was, despite her love of Jones Consulting, she was unhappy with the interference from Franciscan leaders. Franciscan's increasingly challenging workplace culture grew more negative over the last decade. Additionally, Gloria desired to be closer to larger technology hubs, since she longed for new professional challenges. After completing five interviews,

Gloria had offers from four. Only two were serious contenders: a boutique technology firm in downtown Manhattan, and a collaborative think tank just outside the city limits of San Diego.

The two organizations could not be more different. Gloria was drawn to both for different reasons. The boutique technology firm in Manhattan provided an opportunity to conduct research in a technocultural capital of the world, and it was a 75-minute train ride away from Gloria's mother. The team that Gloria would lead was young, driven, and innovative. The team was promoting leading-edge research that helped women entrepreneurs in technology. The firm promised resources that would allow her to conduct research, grow research programs, and continue to support new professionals; however, the think tank in San Diego provided a wholly different culture. The team was collaborative. They were highly engaged in the San Diego technology community. The team often published white papers with one another and community members. Perhaps most important to Gloria, though, was the focus on supporting young professionals; they appeared to value young professionals deeply. The think tank in San Diego was a strong contender for her because it would combine her love of research, engaging with the local community, and focus on mentoring young professionals. For the past few days, Gloria fretted over her impending decision, and her decision deadline was quickly approaching.

As Gloria stepped into her office, she set her bag onto her desk and took out her laptop. "What am I going to do?" she muttered to herself. Both options were appealing to her for entirely different reasons, and each offered her a much-needed change. One thing was for sure, she was leaving Jones Consulting. Despite not knowing where she would land, Gloria knew that she needed to tell her team that she was leaving.

Opening her email, Gloria sent her team a quick note with the subject line: "Weekly meeting moved up to today at 10:30 a.m." This type of email was not uncommon at Jones Consulting; however, most days, the email contained references to whatever doughnuts, pastries, or apple fritters Gloria had brought in from her favorite bakery. Gloria knew that her news would be surprising for her team, but they needed to know. She needed to tell them now.

At the meeting, Gloria told her team about her plans. "Like ripping off a Band-Aid, I have to tell you this because you're my people," she told her team. She grabbed the box of tissues as she saw Lou's eyes begin to water. The team's eyes quickly darted back and forth from one another. It seemed like everyone wanted to say something, but no one did. They sat in a pregnant silence for a minute until Lou finally broke the silence.

"What does this mean for us? What do we do now?" Lou's face reddened as the questions came out too quickly.

Shannon chuckled quietly to herself, and a wide grin spread across her face. "I knew this would happen at some point, Gloria. Lou didn't want to believe it, but I sensed your readiness to make a change. But, I'm with Lou—what does this mean for us and our future with Franciscan? We can certainly tie up loose ends at Jones Consulting, but what about our future work?" Both Shannon and Lou had been on track for promotion within the next few months as they had benefited from Gloria's executive coaching and mentoring.

Gloria smiled, closed her eyes, and took a deep breath. When her eyes opened, Gloria outlined what was to come of her team's next year. She answered Veronica's questions about transitions, who to contact during the transition for questions about Jones Consulting programming. Gloria maintained a cool and collected spirit throughout the meeting, answering questions with ease and assuring her colleagues she would still be available anytime.

After the operational questions were exhausted, Shannon looked at Gloria and said, "I have to ask. I felt this was coming, but why now?"

Gloria leaned back into her chair and responded, "Shannon, I've tried to make changes to Franciscan culture for nearly a decade. It's been very good to me, but I've watched as it has evolved to become more competitive, more political, more fractured as a result, and more negative as we have been asked to do more with less. I want to research, to support young professionals, and feel a sense of family with my colleagues that I once felt. Despite these challenges, I've tried to engage change but kept running into walls . . . " Her voice trailed off as she paused. In that moment as Gloria described what she needed and wanted from her work life, she knew what position was right for her: the think tank in San Diego. Gloria cleared her throat and laughed quietly, "Ahem. Sorry about that. But I just realized which job I'm going to take. It wasn't until I said it out loud that it really hit me—what I need from an organization, its culture, and its people. Thank you, Shannon—it was a really good question!"

"You're welcome—I'm glad that I could help?" Shannon responded, confused.

"Well, Gloria, whoever is next here at Jones Consulting . . . She has big shoes to fill!" Veronica exclaimed. After the meeting, Veronica, Shannon, and Lou began quietly planning a surprise party for Gloria.

Toasting Gloria

"But we're so happy for you. We have been so blessed to have such a wonderful mentor, friend, boss, and leader to work with us. As I told you several months ago, the next director has big shoes to fill. Here's to you, Gloria!" Veronica raised her glass of wine as the crowd matched her toast. Walking to the side of the stage, Veronica handed the microphone to Shannon.

Shannon stepped into the center of the stage as the crowd looked on. "Hi everyone—for those who don't know me, I'm Shannon and I've worked at Jones Consulting for 2 years as research director. I want to echo everything that Veronica has said and build on that to talk about Gloria as a mentor. Gloria is one of the reasons I chose to work at Jones Consulting. As a young professional, I was aware of Gloria's values for both work life and family life. This became especially personal to me when just earlier this year I gave birth to my daughter."

Shannon stopped, and pointed to the back of the room, where her partner was holding their baby. She smiled, and continued, "During this time, I was working part-time as a graduate student with 1 year left, and I was concerned about my ability to finish my degree. Yet, throughout this time, Gloria, you never expressed doubt, assuring me that it would happen. You believed in me and worked closely with me to stay on track and meet deadlines. It is because of you that I know I can complete my degree while working for Jones Consulting, and still be the best mother to my daughter. Gloria, thank you for teaching me to work hard, have faith, and plan for success. You will be missed, but I know I can speak for everyone when I say, we love you and we wish you all the best!" Shannon managed to smile, tears forming in her eyes. "Now I'll turn it over to Lou!" Shannon passed the microphone to Lou, who walked onto the stage.

Taking a deep breath, Lou began, "I'm Lou and I've been at Jones Consulting for a year, and I'm the community engagement director. Many of you probably know me from my emails! I'm not one for making speeches—if you can't tell by my shaky voice!" Lou laughed, and the crowd followed. "Gloria as a mentor, leader, and supervisor really exemplifies someone who is well connected throughout our community! I could always count on you for advice, to help facilitate connections with others, and to be an advocate for and promoter of mine and our team. What I came to realize quickly was not just that you are so well connected, but that your relationships with everyone around the community are meaningful, important, and you make everyone feel important and valued. I look around the room tonight and see your friends, your colleagues, your family all here because of the role that you've played in helping us be successful. So, I . . . " Lou paused for a second before speaking again. "I just want to thank you for being the connector and making us all a priority in your life. We are lucky to have you in our lives, and we're so excited for you!"

Gloria smiled as she wiped the tears from her eyes discreetly, stepping onto the stage. She hugged her team tightly and looked out to the crowd.

"My friends . . . No, my family. Thank you for this wonderful send-off. I . . . " Gloria stopped to look around the room at her family, friends, and colleagues gathered to celebrate her, "I'm truly grateful, and I will miss you all dearly. You are welcome to come visit anytime! There's a place for you in my home. We can have work retreats near my pool!" Gloria raised her glass to the crowd. Everyone toasted to Gloria and clapped as she made her way back to her table.

Although the rest of the evening was a blur for her, as she exited the wine bar later that evening, she was filled with a sense of optimism and excitement. As the summer air comforted her on the way to her car, Gloria smiled as a flood of possibilities swirled around in her head. She looked up to the sky, "What's next?"

DISCUSSION QUESTIONS

1. What kinds of values and assumptions did Gloria associate with Franciscan Consulting Group's culture? In what ways do these values and assumptions align and differ from the organizational culture she desires?

2. What was the organizational exit process like for Gloria? How did her colleagues respond to the news of her exit? How was emotion communicated during this time?

3. If you were Gloria, how would you have shared the news with your colleagues of your new career plans?

4. How do ethics play into Gloria's secrecy around searching for a new job, specifically considering her qualms about Jones Consulting and Franciscan Consulting Group?

5. What kinds of organizational norms were present within Jones Consulting's culture? How might these norms influence how Gloria shared the news of her departure? How might these norms influence how Gloria's colleagues understood and responded to Gloria's news?

SUGGESTED READINGS

Ashcraft, K. L. (2000). Empowering "professional" relationships: Organizational communication meets feminist practice. *Management Communication Quarterly*, *13*, 347–392. https://doi.org/10.1177/0893318900133001

Buzzanell, P. M., Long, Z., Anderson, L. B., Kokini, K., & Batra, J. C. (2015). Mentoring in academe: A feminist poststructural lens on stories of women engineering faculty of color. *Management Communication Quarterly*, *29*, 440–457. https://doi.org/10.1177/0893318915574311

Gardner, W. L., Reithel, B. J., Foley, R. T., Cogliser, C. C., & Walumbwa, F. O. (2009). Attraction to organizational culture profiles. *Management Communication Quarterly*, *22*, 437–472. https://doi.org/10.1177/0893318908327006

Montgomery, B. L. (2017). Mapping a mentoring roadmap and developing a supportive network for strategic career advancement. *SAGE Open*, *7*, 2158244017710288. https://doi.org/10.1177/2158244017710288

TO TALK OR NOT TO TALK: MANAGING UNCERTAINTY WITH COWORKERS

Carrisa S. Hoelscher, PhD
Missouri State University

Mariah stared at the email on her laptop screen, unsure of how to respond. The email was a job offer from her former boss, Luke Hadley, at Woodgrain Markets. He wanted her to come back to her old job . . . and this time he was offering a lot more money and better benefits than she was getting in her current position. "*This is a no-brainer, right?*" she thought to herself. "*Of course I should accept the job.*"

But that meant she would have to leave her current job at Rosen Auto Parts. And that would be hard. She loved her job. Even though she had only been in this position for less than a year, she knew she was happier at Rosen than she had ever been at Woodgrain. Mariah sighed and took another sip of coffee. Still staring at the laptop screen in front of her, she thought back on her career journey since leaving college.

She started her first salaried, full-time job as a graphic designer with Woodgrain Markets just 1 week after graduation. At the time, she was convinced she lucked into her dream job right away. People were typically impressed when she told them she worked for Woodgrain Markets. It was such a staple of the community, providing thousands of jobs and making the area a world-class destination by establishing several restaurants, resorts, shops, and attractions. Everyone knew the name "Woodgrain" and everyone respected the owner, Charlie Thompson—an eccentric, civically engaged, homegrown success. Even if you didn't agree with everything Charlie Thompson did, you

---

This chapter is based on consulting experience.

couldn't argue with how much he helped the local community. And Mariah was proud when she joined his team in the Marketing and Promotions Department at Woodgrain headquarters.

Plus, the job itself seemed glamorous. She was using her graphic design degree, designing all kinds of promotional materials, and she was consistently encouraged to be as creative as she could—any designer's dream!

She specifically remembered an encounter with Luke the first time he asked her to work on designing an invitation for one of Charlie's famous events. Luke sent her a brief note on the office's instant messaging platform: "*Hey Mariah, could you come into my office for a few minutes?*"

Mariah walked down the hall quickly to Luke's office. He didn't even look up from his computer screen as he started talking. "Charlie is holding a reception in a few months to celebrate the opening of a new restaurant just south of town. We want you to work on the invitation design."

Mariah was surprised. Usually newbies didn't get to work on Charlie's events. "Really? That's awesome. I'd love to," she heard herself say.

"Here's the thing," Luke quickly interjected. "Charlie wants 10 different options to choose from, so you need to get started right away. Provide a few traditional options and then be as creative as you want with the others. The sky's the limit!" This time, he looked up and smiled at her. He knew the creative freedom is what typically pushed his designers to work harder.

Mariah asked the first question that comes to every designer's mind, "What's my budget?"

"No budget," Luke replied. "Money is no object when Charlie decides to do an event. But he'll want to see the designs next Wednesday, so get to work."

Mariah could hardly believe what she was hearing. In college, her professors were always talking about the importance of finding a way to let your creativity blossom even when you have limited resources. "In the real world," they loved to say, "you'll always have half the budget you expect." But here she was, in her first "real job," and she was getting to design something using all the resources she could ever want. Mariah went back to her desk, put on her headphones, and got to work on the invitation designs.

Putting on her headphones was a conscious decision. She learned in her first few days on the job that everyone just does that in the Marketing and Promotions Department at Woodgrain Markets: Everyone puts on their headphones and goes to work, mostly working alone for long periods of time and only interacting with one another when absolutely necessary. She didn't mind it so much at first. She enjoyed the quiet solitude in which her creativity could flow. But after a while she noticed herself starting to feel lonely. She tried to engage with coworkers a little more regularly, stopping by their desk with the occasional "How was your weekend?" But they just seemed annoyed by her questions. In fact, one coworker even put a note on her cubicle wall that said, "If I'm wearing my headphones, please don't interrupt me—I'm trying to focus." Mariah got the hint.

Mariah spent a little over a week pouring her heart and soul into 10 different invitation designs. She was so excited to present the options to Charlie himself, since they were for an event he was personally overseeing. When Wednesday morning rolled around, she entered Luke's office: "I am ready to present the options for Charlie's reception invitations! I am really excited to—"

Luke cut her off before she could finish her thought: "Great, just send them to me in an email, and I'll get them where they need to go."

Mariah couldn't help but feel the sting of disappointment. She wouldn't even get to present her designs or hear the feedback on them? Dejectedly, she walked back to her cubicle to send the email, ready to replace the headphones that had become a staple part of her office look. She never heard any feedback on her work and wasn't asked any further questions about the project. But she did catch a glimpse of the final invitation that was sent out a few weeks later: a black-and-white version of one of the traditional, boring designs Mariah included in her 10 options just to appease Luke's request. She was starting to suspect that Charlie never saw her invitation designs at all and Luke just went with the one he wanted, though of course she couldn't prove that.

After several more months of working on projects in this manner, Mariah started to grow weary. She dreaded new projects, dreaded long hours at her desk with her headphones on and little-to-no interaction with those around her, and mostly dreaded never hearing much feedback about her work. While she was always grateful for the seemingly endless resources the department was able to provide her, she soon realized that wasn't enough to keep her happy. She quietly began to look for other jobs.

Just a few weeks later, a job advertisement popped up in her LinkedIn feed: graphic designer for Rosen Auto Parts. She never even thought about how an auto parts store would need a graphic designer. *"What do I know about cars anyway?"* she thought to herself. But she figured it might be worth investigating.

She submitted her resume and found herself sitting in the office of Julie Cox for an interview just a few days later. Julie was the head of the Acquisitions Department, the department that made all of Rosen's newly purchased properties look like all of the other properties in their chain of stores.

Julie was warm and friendly as she described the job to Mariah: "What we're looking for is an experienced graphic designer to work on projects ranging from permanent signage to printed material for store promotions. From the looks of your resume, you'd be able to handle that with no problem at all. I'd love to hear more about your experiences at Woodgrain!"

Mariah found herself chatting comfortably with Julie about her work, occasionally asking some questions about the job at Rosen as well. Finally, she asked the question that had really been on her mind: "What's it really like to work here? How does everyone get along?"

Julie's eyes lit up at this question. "The people here are the absolute best part of my job," she replied. "I know it sounds a bit cliché to say this, but we really are like a family here."

"*Sure*," Mariah thought to herself, picturing the cold and quiet atmosphere at Woodgrain. "*She's just saying that because she has to.*"

Even though she was skeptical, Maria couldn't help but be intrigued. She remembered thinking that it felt more like a conversation with an old friend than an interview.

On the other hand, the job that Julie described didn't sound nearly as glamorous as the one she thought she was accepting with Woodgrain Markets not so long ago. Rosen clearly didn't have access to the same kind of resources that Woodgrain did. And Mariah wouldn't be able to spend her time on creative projects with no restrictions and no budget.

But Julie was so warm and inviting. And when she introduced Mariah to others around the office, everyone seemed genuinely happy to be there. Mariah was even able to hear about how the team collaborated on almost all of their projects. "I work closely with at least six other people on everything I do. I never feel like I'm on my own, which makes it easier for me to take risks and think outside the box," one of the team members told her.

The Marketing and Promotions Department at Woodgrain hardly ever collaborated. Everyone seemed perfectly content to work in cubicle isolation, a feeling represented clearly by the ever-present headphones. Rosen's Acquisitions Department, on the other hand, didn't even have cubicles. Instead, everyone shared one big room, with desks and conference-style tables placed strategically throughout the space. What stuck out to Mariah the most was that everyone was actually talking to each other.

She didn't have to think about that decision very long at the time. She accepted the offer when Julie called the day after her interview.

She gave her 2-weeks' notice at Woodgrain, explaining to Luke that she felt compelled to take this new opportunity to further learn and grow in her career. Luke was polite and understanding, but certainly didn't seem too upset by Mariah's news. "I wish you the best of luck," he said. His terse response made Mariah feel even more confident that she was making the right decision to leave.

Now, she'd been at Rosen for almost a year. Some days she missed the free rein she had with creativity at Woodgrain. And she has definitely had to learn to become more resourceful in her projects at Rosen, given their more restrictive budgets. But she has several new colleagues who are always willing to help pitch in when she is stuck on a certain problem. They almost always seem to accomplish their projects with innovative twists that allow them to maximize what resources they do have— and Mariah was learning to appreciate this new kind of creativity.

What she loved most about her job at Rosen, however, was the relationships she has developed in the department. The department of 12 people, including their boss Julie, was diverse in age, stage of life, education, background, and expertise.

But they all enjoyed working together and even regularly went to lunch or happy hours together. They celebrated birthdays, weddings, and graduations, and helped each other through life's difficult patches as much as they could. She was grateful for her work family and couldn't imagine not seeing them every day. Sure, there were some challenging days, but they tackled those challenges together.

Mariah smiled as she thought of some of the happiest times they all shared at Rosen. But her smile quickly disappeared when the email on the screen caught her eye again. She loved her job, but she couldn't deny how appealing Luke's offer was in the email. He clearly wanted her back at Woodgrain and was offering to almost double her current salary! It felt nice to be pursued and the financial security that Luke was offering was hard to ignore. *"Would the money be worth the job change?"* she asked herself. *"Could I even bear to leave my friends at Rosen?"* Mariah simply didn't know what to do.

DISCUSSION QUESTIONS

1. Mariah was a newcomer at both Woodgrain Markets and Rosen Auto Parts. Using Uncertainty Management Theory as a guide, what types of uncertainties (task, relational, organizational, and/or power) do you think Mariah experienced at each organization?

2. What type of information-seeking strategies and information sources did Mariah use as a means to manage her uncertainty in this case? What other strategies and sources would you recommend to Mariah and why?

3. Mariah's case seems to indicate some differences between her expectations and her experiences being socialized into Woodgrain Markets. Using Louis's (1980) typology of changes, contrasts, and surprises, what kind of discrepancies did Mariah experience?

4. What do you imagine the communication network map would look like for (a) the Marketing and Promotions Department at Woodgrain Markets? and (b) the Acquisitions Department at Rosen Auto Parts?

5. How might you use a communication network approach to explain (a) why Mariah wanted to leave Woodgrain Markets? and (b) why Mariah enjoyed her job so much at Rosen Auto Parts?

6. What evidence do you see of person-job fit and person-organization fit in this case? Which one seems to be more important to Mariah? Which one would be more important for you?

SUGGESTED READINGS

Caldwell, D. F., & O'Reilly, C. A. (1990). Measuring person-job fit with a profile-comparison process. *Journal of Applied Psychology, 75*, 648–657. doi:10.1037/0021-9010.75.6.648

Feeley, T. H., Moon, S. I., Kozey, R. S., & Slowe, A. S. (2010). An erosion model of employee turnover based on network centrality. *Journal of Applied Communication Research, 38*, 167–188. doi:10.1080/00909881003639544

Nifadkar, S. S., & Bauer, T. N. (2016). Breach of belongingness: Newcomer relationship conflict, information, and task-related outcomes during organizational socialization. *Journal of Applied Psychology, 101*, 1–13. doi:10.1037/apl0000035

Saks, A. M., & Gruman, J. A. (2018). Socialization resources theory and newcomers' work engagement: A new pathway to newcomer socialization. *Career Development International, 23*, 12–32. doi:10.1108/CDI-12-2016-0214

Wang, D., Hom, P. W., & Allen, D. G. (2017). Coping with newcomer "hangover": How socialization tactics affect declining job satisfaction during early employment. *Journal of Vocational Behavior, 100*, 196–210. doi:10.1016/j.jvb.2017.03.007

CULTURE AND DECISION MAKING
AT CLAYBORNE RIDGE

David E. Weber, PhD
University of North Carolina, Wilmington

In the middle of the 19th century, Henry Dunant, a young Swiss
executive in the agriculture industry, visited Italy at the request of
the French government. At that time, a war was raging in, what is today,
Northern Italy. One battle ended with almost 40,000 dead, dying, or
wounded soldiers on the battlefield. Observing that panorama of horror, Dunant organized local citizens to treat the casualties and bury
the dead. Dunant began persuading governments of various nations
to sponsor similar war relief efforts and general humanitarian services,
and then to coordinate those efforts across national boundaries. Thus
began the international Red Cross movement, and the American Red
Cross (ARC) emerged in the 1880s.

The national ARC headquarters is in Washington, DC. The 800+
chapters in the United States are grouped into several regions. A chapter receives almost no funding from any level of government—or from
the national headquarters. Instead, it operates primarily from donations made by private citizens and corporations.

The ARC includes over 30,000 paid employees—including the
organization's CEO, executive- and mid-level managers and coordinators, technical or functional professionals, and administrative
specialists—and more than 1 million volunteers. ARC's Board of
Governors includes four dozen attorneys, physicians, academics, public servants, and active or retired business or government leaders. More

This chapter is based on consulting experiences.

than a decade ago, the Board rolled out the following approach to addressing the challenges of measuring how effectively chapters are performing and what to do about those that are not performing well:

- The Board identified criteria by which each chapter will be evaluated and the time limit for submitting evaluations.
- The review process will be conducted out of eight regional offices, with each office responsible for reviewing chapters within a prescribed geographic area.
- The charter of a chapter that does not measure up to performance standards will be targeted for revocation.
- If a chapter's charter is revoked, that chapter must develop a plan to ensure that ARC can continue to serve the chapter's existing and possible future clients.
- Chapters must go through this review and rechartering process every 5 years.

Sandor Parsons, a veteran American Red Cross executive, became the executive officer for the American Red Cross's chapter operations in the Southeast Region. The region consisted of almost 500 local chapters distributed among seven states (North and South Carolina, Tennessee, Georgia, Florida, Alabama, and Mississippi), including large urban chapters as well as tiny rural chapters. After spreading the word that a chapter had to prove it deserved to retain its charter, Parsons distilled the new ARC culture of accountability into three basic principles:

1. Each chapter must do what is right for The American Red Cross in order not to tarnish the image and reputation of ARC.
2. Each chapter must do what is right for those who do, or may, depend on the Red Cross for help. If a community's service needs had not diminished but the chapter's resources have, the chapter has to determine how to meet local needs.
3. If a chapter loses its operating license, its experienced, idealistic, diligent volunteers still had to be kept in the Red Cross family. For example, imagine that a surge in need occurs, such as when a massive hurricane strikes. The Red Cross would need a massive volunteer turnout, even from outside the affected area.

Parsons and his team conducted the chapter evaluation process as follows:

- Parsons plus four staff members served as a first point of contact, meeting with chapter leaders to tell them something like this: "We want you to tell us what your chapter's track record is in performance and service delivery. We're not here to punish you."

- Parsons or his representative distributed self-report instruments to each chapter.
- This team would make itself available as coaches for chapters that were struggling to qualify for charter renewal.

The self-report tools required about 2 weeks to complete. It involved examining compliance with about three dozen requirements for service delivery, leadership and governance, and financial management. The Parsons team digested the self-reports and determined the degree of compliance. If the chapter was in compliance, a renewed charter would be on its way soon thereafter. If the chapter was out of compliance, the team would take the unit through some steps to fix things. Only if a chapter failed to improve would it lose its charter.

One chapter that turned out to be a "problem child" was the Clayborne Ridge chapter. It had a paid full-time staff of seven and a corps of about 90 regular volunteers, and another 50 or so on-call for emergency service. Located in a mountainous part of Parsons's territory, the chapter served a population of about 160,000. Lisa Kopulski served as executive director for a decade, and she had been only recently replaced by Frieda Amory. Amory started out as a volunteer in a large chapter in another state and later moved into paid positions. Kopulski stayed involved in the chapter as an enthusiastic volunteer. Clayborne Ridge's self-report revealed that the chapter missed more than a dozen requirements. Missing just two would have been acceptable. Some of the more noticeable problems that surfaced in the self-report included the following:

- In the biographical summaries about chapter leaders, Wendy Alexander, the chapter's communications and public affairs manager, was identified as a member of the Clayborne Ridge city council. This violated the Red Cross policy of political neutrality among members of a chapter's professional staff.
- The financial section of the self-report showed the chapter was several months in arrears in dues payments to the national office. Dates on financial records accompanying the self-report indicated that the chapter did not provide accurate, timely, and consistent financial information to the national or regional offices.
- Status summaries of chapter services suggested that Clayborne Ridge's programs for disaster preparedness and survivor rescue and relief were below standard.
- Most distressingly—because it was one of the oldest and most respected Red Cross services, and because the military recruited very successfully in the chapter's service area—the report clearly suggested that systems for enabling emergency communication between area families and their loved ones in the armed forces were unreliable.

Parsons contacted Amory to outline some options for remediation. "I'll give you conditional reaccreditation," he offered. "Develop a proposal for hitting the targets you missed. I'll sign off on the proposal if it's solid. Update us every few days with progress reports. When you've made the fixes you propose, we'll convert the conditional charter to a full one."

The proposal came across Parsons's desk by the end of the week. It was superficial, however. So one Thursday, he drove for 3 hours to the chapter to meet with its leadership team, which included Amory, Alexander, Carlo Manelli (assistant executive director), Mel Phillips (the chapter's financial officer), and Petra Granada (director of volunteer and volunteer services).

"I'll give you a 6-month extension," Parsons offered. "And I'll send you a couple of consultants from my staff to help you solve the thorniest problems. We'll do whatever we can to get you through this."

Two of Parsons's associates made a total of five visits to Clayborne Ridge over the next several weeks; each visit lasted 2 or 3 days. Yet no improvements were made in the chapter's operations.

Parsons then contacted the executive director of the Pitchford Chapter, located near Clayborne Ridge. Pitchford had successfully reaccredited. "How about taking Clayborne Ridge under your wing for a month or so?" Parsons asked the director.

The Pitchford leaders agreed to coach Clayborne Ridge personnel for several weeks. At the end of that time, the Pitchford director declared to Parsons, "Frieda is not really steering things there well. She has some sort of 'We don't do it that way down here' thing, and she's kind of intimidated."

Parsons felt torn. On one hand, he knew that ultimately some chapters just do not clear the hurdles to earn reaccreditation, no matter how long you hold their hands. On the other hand, the 6-month extension still had a couple of months left. Perhaps he should let that play out. Of course, the chapter had not yet made any notable headway and Parsons sensed he was devoting too many scarce resources to this one case. Doing so meant he was shorting the hundreds of other chapters he oversaw. He needed to see some tangible results—even minor accomplishments—that suggested the Clayborne Ridge chapter was serious about digging itself out of a hole.

Parsons decided to talk face-to-face with key Clayborne Ridge players. So one October morning, the following people sat in a circle of hard chairs in a small workroom at the chapter building: Parsons; Amory, Kopulski (who Amory called "my consiglieri"), Manelli, Phillips, Alexander, Granada, and Janice Ottoway, a volunteer who coordinated Clayborne Ridge's education programming (e.g., finding instructors and scheduling classes in first aid, CPR, parenting skills, and other topics). Parsons opened the meeting by explaining that in most regions, a chapter that missed the mark by as much as Clayborne Ridge did would not be around even 2 months later.

"Most chapters that fail to meet more than a quarter of the requirements get shut down," Parsons said. "They don't usually get the breathing space I gave you. It's not easy for me to pull the plug, but in 3 months, you haven't moved forward, even with help from a lot of good people. I'm ready to cancel the extension and revoke your charter. But I came up here for you to convince me it would be a mistake to do that—so, you talk, I'll listen."

Chairs squeaked as the meeting participants shifted in them. After some silence, Granada said, "So, let's pretend you've never heard the old saying 'A deal's a deal' and that 6 months doesn't really mean 6 months. What makes you so eager to close us down now instead of 3 months from now?"

Parsons summarized what the consultants and the Pitchford coaches told him. Then, he added, "Apart from that, you still owe a lot of money to the national office. Also, I still need a revision of your plan for disaster response—maybe our most important service. And Wendy, you're still on the city council!"

"Sandor, remember the St. Crispin fire 2 years ago?" Mel Phillips interjected. "That put us almost $15,000 in the hole—made a mess out of our finances." He was referring to a fire in February in Clayborne Ridge's St. Crispin subdivision. He continued, "It destroyed 12 homes and displaced as many families, a total of about 50 people. The $15,000 cost for providing meals and clothing, canned goods, even some toys for the St. Crispin kids represented about 75% of that fiscal year's crisis fund."

Then Carlo Manelli spoke up. "Sandor, this is really only about efficiency, right? The national office wants to close down smaller chapters!"

"Nope," replied Parsons. "National doesn't want to put anyone out of business. They just want each chapter to operate at its full service potential. A good half the chapters in the entire country that have been rechartered thus far are small entities."

"Sandor, I've read those three dozen or so evaluation dimensions, and I wrote a good two-thirds of that self-report," declared Amory. "That evaluation is skewed about 80% toward explaining process administration and only 20% about proven results. But this chapter is all about results—not procedure and hoops to jump through. We have a growing volunteer roster, where most chapters across the country are losing volunteers. Our financial donations have remained steady, but most other chapters have been declining. Wendy designed a campaign to encourage local folks to donate blood. And now blood donations are increasing a bit or remaining steady, while all over the country, blood donations are declining. Janice here has got our rate of completion for basic first aid and CPR classes up to one of the two or three highest of any Red Cross chapter of our size. This chapter's all about getting important stuff done. Maybe we don't dot every 'i,' but we're doing our job."

"No argument from me, Frieda," said Parsons. "I think that's outstanding. The problem is, it's a new game. The national office is saying you have to take that administrative work seriously now. It's not just about getting it done."

"I have something to say," announced Kopulski. She stood up and walked over to a framed document on the wall. She tapped the glass shielding the yellowing paper. "This is our original charter. Dated 1918. Look who signed it: Merle Cochran. Some of you remember Merle—died not even 15 years ago. He himself taught me first aid when I was a kid. In school we'd just learned about atomic weapons and I thought: If they drop an atom bomb on Clayborne Ridge, I can be of some use if I learn first aid. Well, that got me started with the Red Cross.

"I was a volunteer in this chapter in high school. Later, I served as a Red Cross volunteer 'Donut Dolly' with our military in two wars. And I've been on professional staff for 20 years. So I know what I'm talking about when I say that this chapter is not paperwork and dues and facts and figures. This chapter is all about helping our friends here in Clayborne Ridge. That's why most of us are with the Red Cross: We want to help our friends. Sandor, you can't allow us to turn our back on our friends. Give us a chance to continue helping our friends."

The meeting ended shortly thereafter. Parsons promised to reflect overnight on what he would do and to call them the next day with a decision. As he drove the 3 hours back home from this visit to Clayborne Ridge, Parsons asked himself repeatedly, "*What's right for the Red Cross? What's right for Clayborne Ridge clients? What's right for the volunteer base? And how do I make a decision when those principles conflict with one another?*"

DISCUSSION QUESTIONS

1. What are some key internal and external factors that construct Clayborne Ridge chapter's organizational culture?

2. From this case study, what examples can you find of communication constructing the organizational reality of the Clayborne Ridge Red Cross chapter? How may the subculture of the chapter differ from the culture of the larger organization (i.e., the American Red Cross)?

3. Imagine that Sandor Parsons asks you to advise him what to do next. How would persuade him to recharter the Clayborne Ridge chapter? How would you persuade him *not* to recharter the Clayborne Ridge chapter?

4. How would prescriptive (rational) decision-making and alternative decision-making models differ from one another in making a decision on Clayborne Ridge chapter's charter?

5. After reading and digesting this case study, what would you say are a leader's most pressing concerns when making the sort of decision that Sandor Parsons must make regarding either renewing or revoking Clayborne Ridge Red Cross charter?

6. Kidder (as cited in May 2006) has written that ethical dilemmas "don't [necessarily] center on right versus wrong. They center on right versus right" (p. 18). How would you describe the competing ethical considerations that Sandor Parsons must take into account—right-versus-wrong or right-versus-right?

SUGGESTED READINGS

Deetz, S. A., Tracy, S. J., & Simpson, J. L. (2000). *Leading organizations through transition: Communication and cultural change.* Thousand Oaks, CA: Sage.

Eisenberg, E., Andrews, L., Murphy, A., & Laine-Timmerman, L. (1999). Transforming organizations through communication. In P. Salem (Ed.), *Organizational communication and change* (pp. 125–147). Cresskill, NJ: Hampton.

Keyton, J. (2011). *Communication and organizational culture: A key to understanding work experiences* (2nd ed.). Los Angeles, CA: Sage.

May, S. (2006). *Case studies in organizational communication: Ethical perspectives and practices.* Thousand Oaks, CA: Sage.

THE ORGANIZATIONAL CULTURE AND ORGANIZATIONAL ETHICS OF THE NEW YORK YANKEES SURROUNDING ALEX RODRIGUEZ'S DOPING SUSPENSION AND EVENTUAL EXIT

Joshua M. Parcha, PhD
Pennsylvania State University, Hazleton

It was August 5, 2013, and Alex Rodriguez was sitting in the away team's locker room at US Cellular Field in Chicago. He had just been handed a 211-game suspension from Major League Baseball (MLB). The suspension came on accusations from MLB that Rodriguez had used performance-enhancing drugs. At the time, the suspension was the largest given to a player for doping reasons in MLB's history (Eder, 2013).

Rodriguez knew this suspension jeopardized his entire legacy. He was on a 10-year, $275 million contract that was not set to expire until 2017. He was one of the most awarded players in MLB's history: A 14-time American League (AL) All-Star, a 3-time AL Most Valuable Player, and a 10-time AL Silver Slugger. He was the youngest player in MLB history to reach 300, 400, 500, and 600 home runs. Prior to the beginning of the 2013 season, he had accumulated 647 home runs, making him fifth on the all-time home run list (and only 115 home runs away from MLB's all-time home run leader, Barry Bonds). But most significant to Rodriguez about this suspension was that he turned 38 years old just a few days prior. With each MLB season

---

This case study is based on historical events as reported in the news.

containing 162 games, Rodriguez's suspension would cost him nearly 1.5 seasons of baseball—a steep price to pay for a player nearing the end of his career.

"*I wonder if I will ever be able to play baseball again*," Rodriguez probably thought to himself. "*If I have to miss 1.5 years of baseball, I might be too old to play again. The New York Yankees might let me go because hanging on to a 40-year-old baseball player is rare. I need to make sure that I can continue to play. I will fight this suspension.*"

* * * * *

Rodriguez appealed his suspension, and an arbitration hearing was not scheduled until after the 2013 season ended. Rodriguez was relieved to hear that he was to remain playing with the Yankees throughout the rest of the 2013 season. This was significant for Rodriguez because during the remaining part of the 2013 season, Rodriguez hit seven more home runs, slotting him a mere six home runs away from Willie Mays, who was fourth place in all-time MLB career home runs. He also was able to earn the remaining $9 million owed to him that year (Isidore, 2013).

Even though his arbitration was scheduled after the 2013 season, it was still not clear if the Yankees were going to continue to play Rodriguez. After all, if these allegations were true, Rodriguez had engaged in behavior not becoming of a baseball player or of the Yankees organization. However, the Yankees were fighting for a playoff spot, and the Yankee's third-base position would be lacking with the absence of Rodriguez. The Yankees would benefit from continuing to play Rodriguez. As the *New York Times* put it, "Rodriguez is actually lifting the faltering Yankees back into playoff contention" (Sternbergh, 2013, para. 1).

The Yankees decided to play Rodriguez, despite the allegations leveled against him.

How did the fans and his teammates take to him being able to continue to play? In his 2013 *New York Times* article, "Boo Rodriguez or Cheer Him? It's Oh So Complicated," Adam Sternbergh stated that it was hard for Yankees' fans to decide whether to boo or cheer for Rodriguez. They wanted to boo Rodriguez because of his actions in doping, but they also wanted to cheer Rodriguez for his actions in the batter's box.

His teammates seemed to enjoy that the slugger was still allowed to play on their team. Here are some of the comments made by Rodriguez's teammates on his return:

> Derek Jeter (shortstop): "There's so many rumors going on around it, I'm not sure anyone knows what's going on. But he's our teammate. If he's here tomorrow, we look forward to seeing him."
>
> Andy Pettitte (pitcher): "If the guy comes back and he's healthy, he can help this team win. I think he can help us. Everything that comes after that, we'll have to wait and see." (Waldstein, 2013a)

From the Yankees organization's perspective, playing Rodriguez for the remaining part of the 2013 season was a positive. The fans still came to the stadium, and the team as a whole had a better chance of winning. Rodriguez helps the Yankees win, so innocent until proven guilty, right?

Other teams were less receptive that Rodriguez was allowed to continue playing. For example, consider what John Lackey, a pitcher at the time for the Boston Red Sox, said of Rodriguez: "I've got a problem with it. You bet I do. How is he still playing? He obviously did something and he's playing. I'm not sure that's right" (Kepner, 2013, para. 11).

It is hard to determine what Lackey actually values. Does he value *fair play*, or does he value *team success*? The Yankees value *team success*, so it makes sense to continue to play Rodriguez. However, the Red Sox are rivals with the Yankees, arguably the most intense rivalry in all of sports. From Lackey's statement, it seems like he values *fair play*, but with Rodriguez out of the Yankees' lineup, the Red Sox have a much better chance of winning games against the Yankees.

✳ ✳ ✳ ✳ ✳

It had been over a week since Rodriguez's suspension. Brian Cashman, the Yankees general manager, was watching the Yankees play against the Red Sox at Fenway Park. He struggled to know how exactly to deal with the Rodriguez scandal. Much like the Yankee fans, he called Rodriguez a "liar and [said] he no longer trusted Rodriguez enough to discuss any substantive matters with him. Yet when Rodriguez is in the batter's box, Cashman [found himself rooting] hard for him to succeed" (Waldsten, 2013b, para. 1).

Maybe the thought process for Cashman was simple: Rodriguez's doping scandal is making such headlines only because Rodriguez is such a high-profile player. There are surely many other MLB players who are doping and have not been caught. Maybe one day doping will be an accepted tradition in professional sports, and we will not be having this conversation anymore.

However, doping is—for the time being at least—frowned upon and punished in professional sports today. If Cashman truly thought that Rodriguez was a liar, it was peculiar that he continued to allow him to play. But in sports organizations, exceptions are made, especially for the most popular sports figures. If Rodriguez was not a good player and on a low-salary contract, there is little doubt that he would have been treated differently.

✳ ✳ ✳ ✳ ✳

Rodriguez was not allowed to play during the entire 2014 season. Through arbitration, the original 211-game suspension was lowered to 162 games. Although the final suspension was less severe, it was still—at the time—the largest suspension given to an MLB player in regards to doping.

Rodriguez returned to playing baseball for the 2015 season and part of the 2016 season. His lack of batting success was beginning to become a liability for the

Yankees. At times, there were at-bats that reminded everyone of the baseball player that Rodriguez was in the past. However, his batting average dipped to .200 during the 2016 season, making him no longer productive enough for the Yankees to keep playing him regularly.

Almost 3 years from the date of the initial suspension, Rodriguez decided to retire from baseball. "This is a tough day," he said at his press conference. "I love this game and I love this team, and today I'm saying goodbye to both." The Yankees and Rodriguez had mutually come to an agreement that retirement was the best option at this point for both the Yankees and Rodriguez (Hoch, 2016).

Leaders in the Yankees organization praised Rodriguez. Hal Steinbrenner, one of the Yankee owners, said, "Baseball runs through his blood. He's a tireless worker and an astute student of the game. Alex has already proven to be a willing and effective mentor to many players who have come through our clubhouse, and I am confident that this next phase of his baseball life will bring out the best in Alex and the next generation of Yankees." Cashman praised Rodriguez's baseball I.Q., and how winning the 2009 World Series happened in part because they had Rodriguez on their team (Hoch, 2016).

Despite retiring from the game he loved, things were still looking up for Rodriguez. He was still paid the remaining amount of his contract that was owed to him. He also began working for the Yankees organization as a special advisor.

Rodriguez will most likely never make it into MLB's Hall of Fame due to this doping scandal. Yet post retirement, Rodriguez has been given many opportunities to repair his image. He has been a guest shark on ABC's Shark Tank, is an MLB Analyst at FOX Sports, and also calls baseball games on ESPN's "Sunday Night Baseball." He is CEO of A-ROD Corporation, an investment company. His baseball career earnings—nearly $450 million—have provided Rodriguez with plenty of financial assets needed to run this corporation (http://www.spotrac.com/mlb/new-york-yankees/alex-rodriguez-597/cash-earnings/).

✷ ✷ ✷ ✷ ✷

As Rodriguez left the playing field for the last time as a player on August 12, 2016, he made sure to take some of the infield dirt from Yankee Stadium with him. He probably thought of all the good—and challenging—memories baseball would leave him. Baseball had a great player in Rodriguez for the 22 years that he played. His legacy, however, will be clouded by that fateful day on August 5, 2013—a day that changed Rodriguez's life, the New York Yankees, and MLB forever.

DISCUSSION QUESTIONS

1. When Cashman calls Rodriguez a liar, but also roots for him to succeed, what conflicting values are at play? Do you think the New York Yankees organization as a whole has conflicting values? Why or why not?

2. What similar conflicting values might be present in other organizations outside of MLB? Have you experienced conflicting values at your work?
3. Besides professional sports organizations, how might top employees in other occupations get away with unethical behavior?
4. When Rodriguez retired midway through the 2016 season, what reasons would you give to consider this retirement (a) an involuntary exit, (b) a voluntary exit, or (c) a coerced exit?
5. What are some of the costs and benefits of allowing a top employee to continue working for an organization even after he or she has done something unethical?
6. When do you think is it appropriate to dismiss a top employee immediately?

REFERENCES

Eder, S. (2013, August 5). M.L.B. Suspends Rodriguez and 12 Others for Doping. *The New York Times*. Retrieved from http://www.nytimes.com/2013/08/06/sports/baseball/mlb-suspends-12-in-doping-investigation.html

Hoch, B. (2016, August 7). A-Rod to Play Final Game Friday, Become Yanks Advisor. *MLB.com*. Retrieved from https://www.mlb.com/yankees/news/alex-rodriguez-to-retire/c-194038578

Isidore, C. (2013, August 5). Suspension Could Cost A-Rod $31 Million. *CNN Money*. Retrieved from http://money.cnn.com/2013/08/05/news/companies/a-rod-lost-pay/index.html

Kepner, T. (2013, August 16). Rodriguez Offers Support, but Finds Little in Return. *The New York Times*. Retrieved from http://www.nytimes.com/2013/08/17/sports/baseball/as-rodriguez-plays-on-others-voice-displeasure.html

Sternbergh, A. (2013, August 27). Boo Rodriguez or Cheer Him? It's Oh So Complicated. *The New York Times*. Retrieved from http://www.nytimes.com/2013/08/28/sports/baseball/boo-alex-rodriguez-or-cheer-him-for-a-yankees-fan-its-complicated.html

Waldstein, D. (2013a, August 4). Rodriguez Is Expected to Play While Appealing Suspension. *The New York Times*. Retrieved from https://www.nytimes.com/2013/08/05/sports/baseball/rodriguez-is-expected-to-play-while-appealing-suspension.html?_r=0

SUGGESTED READINGS

Dougherty, D., & Smythe, M. J. (2004). Sensemaking, organizational culture, and sexual harassment. *Journal of Applied Communication Research*, *32*, 293–317. doi.org/10.1080/0090988042000275998

Jovanovic, S., & Wood, R. V. (2006). Communication ethics and ethical culture: A study of the ethics initiative in Denver city government. *Journal of Applied Communication Research*, *34*, 386–405. doi.org/10.1080/00909880600908633

Lucas, K., & Fyke, J. P. (2014). Euphemisms and ethics: A language-centered analysis of Penn State's sexual abuse scandal. *Journal of Business Ethics*, *122*, 551–569. doi.org/10.1007/s10551-013-1777-0

Lyon, A. (2007). "Putting patients first": Systematically distorted communication and Merck's marketing of Vioxx. *Journal of Applied Communication Research, 35,* 376–398. doi.org/10.1080/00909880701611052

Ploeger, N. A., Kelley, K. M., & Bisel, R. S. (2011). Hierarchical mum effect: A new investigation of organizational ethics. *Southern Communication Journal, 76,* 465–481. doi.org/10.1080/1041794x.2010.500343

Waldstein, D. (2013b, August 18). More Friction between Yankees and Rodriguez. *The New York Times.* Retrieved from http://www.nytimes.com/2013/08/19/sports/baseball/more-friction-between-yankees-and-rodriguez.html

MAKING SENSE OF CHANGING RELATIONSHIPS WITH THE BOSS AND PEERS

Jaesub Lee, PhD
University of Houston

J ane and Stacy started their jobs in Corporate America together about 3 years ago. During a new employee orientation that lasted all day, they sat right next to each other and chatted about many little things, such as weather, hobbies, movies, and previous jobs. They felt good about each other and became friends. They've kept in touch frequently through email, texting, and calling. Eventually, they considered each other best friends.

They worked in different departments, which were housed in different buildings. Stacy worked in Accounting and Jane in Customer Service. After work, they often spent time together at shopping malls, bars, events, and venues. When Jane went through a difficult medical procedure, Stacy was there supporting and cheering her up all the time with bright flowers and funny stories beside her hospital bed. After the operation, they felt very close to each other and, with a deep sense of bonding, became best friends.

Stacy was somewhat concerned about Jane lately. For the last few get-togethers, Jane looked a little defeated and uncertain about herself.

This chapter is based on published work: Lee, J., Lim, J. J. C., & Heath, R. L. (2017). Coping with workplace bullying through NAVER: Effects of LMX relational concerns and cultural differences. *International Journal of Business Communication*. doi:10.1177/2329488417735649

She had somewhat darkish circles around her eyes and looked preoccupied. She also seemed to lose her temper quickly and get easily irritated.

Stacy asked, "What's going on with you, lately?"

"Just mind your own business," snapped Jane. "You don't have to care about me. I can take care of myself."

Stacy was taken aback. That was definitely not what Stacy expected from her best friend. She figured something must be going on that Jane did not want to talk about. She decided to give her some space. So she left it at that.

Nonetheless, worried about Jane, the next day during lunch hour, Stacy dropped by Jane's department to see how she was doing. Stacy didn't see her and was told that Jane was absent from work that day. The same thing happened the next day—no Jane at work. Alarmed and uneasy, Stacy called her at home to ask what was going on. Jane was reluctant to say anything. She simply stated that she was a little sick for the last few days.

But Stacy asked more questions, "Where does it hurt? Did you go see a doctor? Are you taking any medicine? Is there something I can do for you? Do you need a ride?"

Jane insisted that she was okay, just a little bit tired. She demanded that Stacy not worry, adding, "I just don't feel like doing much right now. I just don't feel good about myself. I will be fine by tomorrow. I promise I will be back tomorrow and talk to you."

Stacy let it go at that and concluded, "I hope you feel better soon."

Tomorrow came; again Jane was nowhere to be seen at work. Hoping that Jane may show up later, Stacy stayed at work until the end of day, visiting her department every couple of hours or so. Jane never showed; very worried and very troubled, Stacy drove some 40 miles to Jane's place.

After much prodding from Stacy, and with a glass of wine in her hand, Jane spoke. "Stacy, I have been a great employee. I am really good at what I do. My job performance is great. I've won a few awards for exceptional accomplishments. I was an Employee of the Month a few months ago. I also received the Customer Service Award last year. The senior management said that I will be put on the 'fast track' and may be the first one to get promoted in my department. Being an outstanding performer, I somehow sensed the very source of my problems I am having now. You see, I heard my supervisor, Dan, was reprimanded for his personal conduct with a very important customer."

She continued, "It all started when I logged into my computer a few months ago. You see, I couldn't find several customer accounts, in fact, my most high-profile accounts. I searched and searched for my precious accounts everywhere in the computer. I even called IT folks to help me but to no avail. I was in panic mode and ran to Dan's office to explain what happened and ask for help. Even without hearing the whole story, he told me he already knew what happened. In fact, he said he removed my accounts and gave them to another customer service rep. I was sort of dumbfounded. I asked why. I said, 'I've worked so hard to build those customer accounts, spending hours to build rapport and trust with customers.' I told him that he can't do that. 'They are my customers. I don't believe you can' . . . He cut me off and simply said that 'I made the decision so that everyone in the department benefits the most.' I couldn't believe what I was hearing. I raised my voice for the injustice of his decision and said, 'You don't even have the common courtesy to talk to me or inform me of the decision beforehand? And I had to find out the hard way? I can't believe you are my' . . . Dan, again, interrupted me before I finished my words and said in an angry tone of voice 'I am your supervisor. You take it or leave it. Well, in fact, you can leave. You're not really valued here anyway.'"

"This was bad, really bad. Just within one quick conversation, I felt my life flashed from best employee to a worthless one. What's more concerning, I felt my job was in danger. From this moment on, everything with Dan went downhill. I couldn't stomach his unilateral decision making. It wasn't like that at all for the last 2 years. In fact, he has been very helpful, guiding me in many ways. I was a great student of his. After this encounter, I lost some confidence in my people skills. I mean, I was supposed to be one heck of an expert in relational matters. I feel lost here. I am clueless about what is going on."

With a heavy dose of encouragement and moral support from Stacy, Jane found enough inner strength to return to work the next day. Nevertheless, she couldn't help but thinking about what really happened. As she pondered preceding events, she began to nod her head here and there, muttering "*hmms*," "*could be*," and "*perhaps*." She debated and debated all sorts of things in her mind. Finally, she decided to make some inquiries. In the following days, with her spirit somewhat refreshed and an attitude of "*There's got to be a reasonable explanation somewhere,*" she talked with a few coworkers. Her peers have served as eyes and ears to each other, sharing any useful information, such as a new policy on customer parking, training etiquette in customer calling, management guidelines about working on customer accounts, and the like. She asked pretty much the same questions to all of her peers.

She asked, for example, "What's the scoop lately? Is there something I need to be aware of? Was there some new policy on accounts?" However, at first, the grapevine didn't provide much new information. It appeared to her things were as normal as they can be.

Finally, Jane revealed to two peers, who she felt she could trust a little more than others, that Dan took her most important accounts and gave them to others.

They were surprised, asking, "Really? Why? "I know you've worked so hard to get your accounts going. That is unbelievable. It's just unfair."

Jane continued, "I have no clue as to why he did it. Did you hear anything about some rep getting more accounts lately?"

They both said, "Not really. But there was a vague rumor going on that the recent hire is from Dan's hometown. She may be Dan's relative or something."

Jane said to herself, "Aha!" With this revelation, Jane realized that Dan was playing favorites.

But the most drastic turning point in her relationship with Dan took place when Jane was called into his office. As soon as Jane sat down, Dan angrily accused her of not respecting his directives, "You never follow up on anything. You didn't include updated information in the email. What's your problem?"

Jane responded shakily, "I listed all the updates in the previous email and all emails today when you asked me to include any information about my new customers."

"I am so busy. I don't have time to read. You just can't email me all the time."

"I see. I will . . ."

Interrupting her, Dan said, "Apparently, you're not up to the task. You never get anything done right here. You're not trying hard enough. You are basically lazy and incompetent. I don't see anything worthwhile in your work. You apparently don't care about your work or the organization. Why should I keep you here?"

Jane was speechless.

Dan continued, now shouting, "Do you hear me? You're lazy and stupid. I don't want to see your face! Get out of here!"

Jane ran out of the room with a tear hanging in her eyes.

DISCUSSION QUESTIONS

1. Jane's relationship with the boss has transformed from good to bad rather drastically. Discuss the change from the perspective of leader-member exchange theory. Speculate how communication behaviors impact the leader-member exchange quality, and vice versa.

2. Jane and Stacy are best friends. Sketch how they have become best friends from mere acquaintances at the new employee orientation. Tell your "transitional story" on becoming the best friend to someone at work.

3. To what extent do you believe Jane's attempts to make sense of what's going on are effective (e.g., discovering and giving meaning to what's taking place)? Are Jane's sensemaking efforts consistent with Weick's sensemaking principles?

4. How common is bullying at your workplace? Identify specific verbal and nonverbal behaviors that represent workplace bullying in the case or in your experience. What makes these behaviors unethical?

5. What sorts of intervention program for workplace bullying would you like to see in place?

6. Jane experienced emotional turmoil. Discuss Jane's *emotion with work* and *emotion toward work*.

SUGGESTED READINGS

Einarsen, S., Hoel, H., & Notelaers, G. (2009). Measuring exposure to bullying and harassment at work: Validity, factor structure and psychometric properties of the

Negative Acts Questionnaire-Revised. *Work & Stress, 23,* 24–44. doi:10.1080/02678370902815673

Einarsen, S., Hoel, H., Zapf, D., & Cooper, C. L. (Eds.). (2011). *Bullying and harassment in the workplace: Developments in theory, research, and practice* (2nd ed.). Boca Raton, FL: Taylor & Francis.

Graen, G. B., & Uhl-Bien, M. (1995). Relationship-based approach to leadership: Development of leader-member exchange (LMX) theory of leadership over 25 years: Applying a multi-level multi-domain perspective. *Leadership Quarterly, 6,* 219–247. doi:10.1016/1048-9843(95)90036-5

Kram, K. E., & Isabella, L. A. (1985). Mentoring alternatives: The role of peer relationships in career development. *Academy of Management Journal, 28,* 110–132. doi:10.2307/256064

Lee, J. (2005). Communication as antecedents and consequences of LMX development globally: A new strong inference approach. In G. B. Graen (Ed.), *New frontiers of leadership: Global organizing designs* (Vol. 3, pp. 1–41). Greenwich, CT: Information Age.

Lee, J., Lim, J., & Heath, R. L. (2017). Coping with workplace bullying through NAVER: Effects of LMX relational concerns and cultural differences. *International Journal of Business Communication.* doi:10.1177/2329488417735649

Namie, G. (2014). *2014 WBI U.S. workplace bullying survey.* Bellingham, WA: Workplace Bullying Institute. Retrieved from http://www.workplacebullying.org/wbiresearch/wbi-2014-us-survey/

Sias, P. M. (2009). *Organizing relationships: Tradition and emerging perspectives on workplace relationships.* Thousand Oaks, CA: Sage.

Sias, P. M., & Cahill, D. J. (1998). From coworkers to friends: The development of peer friendships in the workplace. *Western Journal of Communication, 62,* 273–299. doi:10.1080/10570319809374611

Tye-Williams, S., & Krone, K. J. (2015). Chaos, reports, and quests: Narrative agency and co-workers in stories of workplace bullying. *Management Communication Quarterly, 29,* 3–27. doi:10.1177/0893318914552029

Weick, K. E. (1995). *Sensemaking in organizations.* Thousand Oaks, CA: Sage.

16

CHANGING FROM ONE COACH TO ANOTHER

MANAGING LEADERSHIP CHANGES

Sophie Moll, BA
University of Oklahoma

Michael W. Kramer, PhD
University of Oklahoma

Cassie was thrilled when she found out she was one of the few ninth graders to make the Stapleton High School women's varsity soccer team. A dedicated soccer player, she attended every varsity match for 7 years, wondering what it would be like to be on the team. She idolized SHS players and marveled at their skills. She noticed the players seemed to have an unrelenting devotion to their teammates and a passion for the sport whether or not they had a successful season. She could see they were a close-knit group by the way they supported each other on the sidelines whether they made a good play or a poor one. At homecoming each year, there seemed to be a bond between returning players even years after graduating. She also noticed how community members, not just players' parents, were loyal, enthusiastic supporters of one of the region's best women's high school soccer programs.

What Cassie observed was quite different than her experience playing on local competitive-league soccer teams for several years. On those teams, the main priority seemed to be individual success with no real concern for loyalty or friendship. Her coaches emphasized, "You

This case study is based on the first author's experiences in high school and was initially developed for a class assignment related to Chapter 13 of Kramer & Bisel, 2017. 13.

need to be better than your teammates if you're going to make the high school team." That meant players rarely developed friendships, unless they attended the same school. And the community took no interest in those teams; only parents watched games. Competitive-league teams were just training grounds for the real team, the SHS varsity team.

Cassie immediately knew things were different on the SHS team. From the first meeting, Coach Jason Lucas stressed, "We win as a team and we lose as a team." In practice, he criticized players who tried to score on their own instead of passing to an open player. And his message worked. The women played selflessly compared to her competitive-league teams. They passed to open players because they did not care who scored as long as the team scored.

During the fall, Cassie learned what it meant to be a rookie, a newbie, trying to become part of the close-knit team of veteran players. Because she wanted to fit in, she observed carefully to try to figure out important team norms. She learned one at the second practice when Jordan, a senior, took her aside and said, "I know practice officially starts at 3:00, but if you want to become a starter and impress Coach, you'll be here at least 10 minutes early." After that Cassie was warming up 15 minutes before practice and some players were always already there.

There were other norms that didn't seem so important, but to fit in, Cassie tried to imitate them. For example, during school, players always acknowledged one another in the hall and sat together in class, if the teacher did not assign seats. At practice, they played aggressively, but safely so no one got injured.

Cassie noticed that if there wasn't a game on Friday, the older players went out to eat together after practice at the local pizza joint. Cassie envied their friendship. Then after about 2 weeks of practice, Jordan caught her after practice one Friday and asked, "Why don't you join us? I can give you a ride home if you need one." Cassie was so excited when she texted her mom that she would not be home for dinner; her mother understood how important this was to her and texted back "Congratulations."

It didn't surprise Cassie that practices involved hard work, or that players were supportive of each other, especially once she and other newbies demonstrated they contributed to the team. What really surprised Cassie was Coach Lucas. From watching him on the sidelines, she thought he was an intimidating, stern man. She figured he did not have close attachments to any of the players and ran a tight ship. From the stands, she always wondered how the players were so cohesive when their coach acted like a dictator on the sidelines. He seemed to be all business as he barked out orders for substitutes and admonished players when they misplayed the ball or when he chided a referee for a blown call, although never in a disrespectful way.

Cassie learned that Coach Lucas behaved quite differently away from competition. To her surprise, team members were part of some decisions. For example, after a loss, at the next practice, he would gather all the players and ask, "Why do you think we lost?" The players would offer suggestions like "We waited too long to pass" or "We kept playing the right side, their strong side. We needed to attack the left." Then, Coach Lucas would develop drills for practice to emphasize one-touch passing or give extra praise every time they played to the left during scrimmage. The game plan for the next match would be based on what the players contributed. At some practices, he would simply ask, "What should we work on today?" He would select drills based on their suggestions.

Involving players in decisions made everyone accountable for their choices and actions; they understood they were responsible for the game's outcome. Involving them in decisions emphasized the importance of positive team relationships by promoting cooperation on and off the field. Not only did this make them more productive during matches, but it created those supportive and committed relationships that Cassie saw lasting after players finished their careers. After 2 months, Cassie realized participating in decisions and developing positive relationships truly drove the team's success, as much as the goal of winning. Coach Lucas's open communication created respect, allegiance, and loyalty to the team and to him as the coach.

Coach Lucas reinforced his open relationship by having players call him "CJay." This nickname contrasted with Cassie's image of an authoritative, directive coach pacing the sidelines. It showed he had well-formed, positive relationships with each team member. Rather than taking advantage of this, team members responded with diligence and respect by listening and taking directions during practice and matches. This was a stark contrast to Cassie's experiences on her competitive-league teams.

CJay used certain rituals to reinforce his ideals. For example, a ritual before each match was a team dinner at someone's house. CJay would sit at the head of the table and tell stories of his time as a soccer player. He loved to tell the story of his high school state final game:

"It was tied with about 2 minutes left in regulation time. Suddenly, we drove down the field with one last chance to score. I got a pass in the middle of the field. Their players were tired, but they started closing in on me. I saw my friend, Carson, charging down the right side and Philip a few steps farther back on the left side. I faked to Carson. The defenders and goalie took the bait. Then I passed to Philip. The goalie was out of position. He had an open shot. Goooooooooalll!"

Not only did players love to hear him tell this and others stories, but the stories reinforced the team culture he valued. He would also ask for feedback on how things were going. Then he always managed to relate the topics to a pregame pep talk.

His commitment and passion for the program were also apparent after every game. Win or lose, he mobilized parents to meet at a nearby local restaurant, Wrights, after the game. Not only was he dedicated to his players, but he took time out of his personal life to socialize with parents and thank them for their support and ask for their feedback on any changes they believed were needed.

Unfortunately, that all changed after a big match 3 months into the season. Cassie remembered CJay pulling her aside after that Friday match. He gave her what would be his last pep talk to her, "Cassie, you played hard tonight. Don't let up. Push yourself. If you do, you'll become a team leader. If you keep working hard, the freshman will be looking up to you like you look up to Jordan."

The next morning, Cassie took CJay's words to heart and went on an extra-long conditioning run. When she finished, there were multiple messages from her closest teammate and other players on her phone. CJay was in a horrible accident that night. His chances of recovering were considered slim.

The players met at school to wait. Everyone was there. They tried to be optimistic. They repeated certain things over and over in between small talk.

"Doctors can do amazing things these days. They'll fix this."

"CJay is a fighter. He'll pull through."

Later that evening Tracy, the team captain, got the call from the athletic director. CJay had passed away. The players tried to console each other, but they were devastated.

The players were excused from school for the next 2 days. They met at Jordan's house and watched movies, slept, and grieved. Two days was not enough time.

It seemed like the entire community turned out for the funeral held at the large Methodist church in the next town to accommodate everyone. Wright's catered the reception in the fellowship hall, where a long line of former and current players, students, parents, teachers, and community members waited to give their condolences to the Coach's wife, the SHS softball coach. To say the death of CJay was a shock to the community was an understatement. More personally, Cassie and the other players felt the sporadic emotions tied to mourning the loss of a friend and mentor for a long time. His death instantly altered the soccer program.

In an attempt to keep the program going, the school's athletic director and head football coach, Terry Anderson, made an executive decision, without any input from the players, that he and an assistant coach would coach women's soccer. He held a short meeting with the players the Monday after the funeral and simply announced his decision: "Most of you know me as the football coach. I'm also athletic director. I know this is a difficult time for you, but we want to make the best of it and keep the program going. Since there isn't time to find a new coach until next season, I've decided I'm going to be your new coach. Coach Nicholson will assist me. Practice will be at the same time beginning tomorrow. We have a game on Saturday. Any questions?"

The players were still in shock and also surprised by this decision. No one managed to ask a question, and Coach Anderson seemed to prefer it that way. After a brief pause, he added, "See you tomorrow," and left.

Practices changed immediately. Coach Anderson did not seem to know anything about soccer. He knew strength and conditioning. His drills might help players become stronger, but they did not do anything to improve their soccer skills. It seemed like they rarely used the ball except during scrimmages. Players missed CJay's drills that actually helped them during games.

They missed being able to suggest what they should work on in practice. Coach Anderson made all the decisions. They missed CJay's emphasis on being a team and building positive relationships rather than only on winning. When the players got together, they complained.

"Do these stupid drills have anything to do with soccer?"

"Does he know anything about soccer?"

"He's an idiot."

"If only . . ."

Cassie realized team spirit had changed dramatically. Players perceived their passion came from CJay; without CJay they felt lost. Coach Anderson's formal relationship with them did not help. He insisted they address him as Coach Anderson instead of as CT. They didn't feel they could talk to him. During the first weeks under new leadership, players rejected the new coaches by not responding to the few times they were asked for input and by not responding verbally to anything but the simplest requests. Even though the new coaches told the players to go about the regular practice schedule, Cassie noticed that no one showed up early anymore and players sometimes even skipped practices. Cassie missed the pregame dinner ritual when it stopped, too. It wasn't that the players discussed their behaviors with each other; it just seemed like everyone thought if they ignored the changes, things might return to normal, even though they knew that was impossible. The new coaches tried to be sensitive to the players' loss by overlooking their misbehaviors. And besides, they were busy with football anyway.

Players talked about quitting or at least not playing next year. When the team forfeited a couple of games, Cassie recognized that something needed to change, but she felt powerless as a newcomer to do anything. She remembered the moment things started to change.

A couple of seniors called a players-only team meeting. When everyone was there, the captain, Tracy, gave a powerful talk. She began, "I realize that you are all heartbroken about the loss of CJay." She had to pause to fight back emotions, but then continued: "We can't continue like we are, ignoring the coaches and skipping practices. It's already hurting us. I mean, we've already forfeited two games. It's not going to get better unless we change. I mean, Coach Anderson isn't going to go away, at least not this year. We've got to start listening to him and cooperating or the whole season will be lost. And here's the really important thing. CJay would be really disappointed in us if he saw us now. He taught us to work hard, to support each other through good times and bad. Well, this is a bad time, but we can get through it together. We can make him proud by pulling together and supporting each other. I'll be at practice early tomorrow."

Cassie noticed there weren't many dry eyes in the room, including her own. But then she spoke up for the first time at a team meeting, "We have a game Saturday. Friday night I'm inviting you all over for dinner. It won't be the same without CJay, but . . ." She couldn't finish the sentence, but it didn't matter. There was a chorus of

"I'll be there" and "Count on me." It wasn't clear if they were talking about practice or dinner.

The next day, everyone arrived for practice early. Coach Anderson seemed surprised everyone was already practicing when he showed up at 3:15. Jordan spoke for the team.

"CT, practice starts at 3:00. Where were you?"

DISCUSSION QUESTIONS

1. What communication experiences assisted Cassie in joining the team and crossing organizational boundaries?
2. Many different people demonstrated managerial and organizational leadership throughout the case. Analyze each one. How did each one use artifacts, rituals, assumptions, and communication norms to influence others?
3. The players appeared to go through the stages of grief both for the loss of their coach and for the resulting changes. Provide evidence for both.
4. The players resisted change. Was their resistance effective or ineffective? Do their actions seem appropriate considering the circumstances?
5. What characteristics of systems theory are evident in the interactions of the soccer team and the community?
6. Was it appropriate for Coach Anderson to name himself soccer coach?

SUGGESTED READINGS

Deal, T. E. (1985). Cultural change: Opportunities, silent killer, or metamorphosis? In R. Kilmann, M. Saxton, & R. Serpa (Eds.), *Gaining control of corporate culture* (pp. 292–331). San Francisco, CA: Jossey-Bass.

Kast, F. E., & Rosenzweig, J. E. (1972). General systems theory: Applications for organization and management. *Academy of Management Journal, 15,* 447–465.

Van Maanen, J., & Schein, E. G. (1979). Toward a theory of organizational socialization. In B. M. Staw (Ed.), *Research in organizational behavior* (pp. 209–264). Greenwich, CT: JAI Press.

Zoller, H. M. (2014). Power and resistance in organizational communication. In L. L. Putnam & D. K. Mumby (Eds.), *The SAGE handbook of organizational communication: Advances in theory, research, and methods* (3rd ed., pp. 595–618). Los Angeles, CA: Sage.

ONE OF US?

EXAMINING ORGANIZATIONAL LEADERSHIP AND DECISION MAKING THROUGH (NON) ETHICAL ORGANIZATIONAL POLICIES

Benjamin D. Luttrull, BA
University of Southern Indiana

Jessica M. Rick, PhD
University of Southern Indiana

Kaleb, a 22-year-old communication studies major, put on earbuds and started the walk home from campus after an unexpectedly concerning meeting of his fraternity, Iota Alpha Eta (IAH), one of the biggest and most respected social Greek fraternities in the country. Kaleb's chapter, Rho Mu, however, was not as reflective of that tradition—the chapter was placed on probation by the national fraternity. Kaleb had just been re-elected chapter president after helping the chapter reform and get back in good standing. Now, that good standing was about to be complicated again, and Kaleb was hoping to use his walk home to think.

The meeting in question was a meeting of the class of prospective members. They were collectively about halfway done with their education process, which meant they only had about 6 weeks before their full initiation. This pledge class was one for the ages in terms of both quality and quantity and was led by Paul, someone who everyone had already pegged as a future chapter president because of his fire for the

This case is based on the first author's personal experience as a regional advisor of a social fraternity.

group and his obvious leadership talent. Other fraternities on campus were recruiting Paul heavily, so his presence in the chapter would solidify the chapter's turnaround as an organization of good repute.

After the class meeting, however, Paul asked to meet with Kaleb and two other chapter leaders privately. Once alone, Paul painstakingly revealed that he was transgender and that while he had started transitioning before coming to college, the application to change his driver's license hadn't been fully processed by the state. Paul then produced his driver's license, which had an "F" under the Sex designation and his pretransition, female name, Sarah. He asked the brothers to keep this confidential but felt obligated to share because of his uncertainty of how it affected the education process.

Kaleb left this meeting stunned and with a sinking feeling in his gut. As he walked home, he recalled hearing from other chapters in the region that there was a transgender policy adopted by IAH Nationals. When he got back to his apartment, Kaleb pulled out his governing documents and searched for the exact wording of the policy. It was the shortest policy in the binder, but it was efficiently worded:

POLICY ON TRANSGENDER MEMBERS: Iota Alpha Eta is a social fraternity for men who seek to better themselves and their communities. The Fraternity defines a man as someone who is legally and medically male. Legal status is determined by state government-issued identification, where medical status is determined by the written consent of a primary-care physician.

"Great," Kaleb muttered out loud after shutting his binder and throwing it on his bed. The chapter had made it pretty clear that one of the reasons they respected him was his willingness to hold people accountable when they went against the bylaws, and that accountability was a large reason for the chapter's rehabilitation. Now, the bylaws were telling him that one of the best potential members the chapter had recruited in a long time wasn't eligible for membership on what Kaleb considered a technicality. He couldn't understand why anyone would have an issue with Paul, but rules are rules.

After a couple minutes of thinking, Kaleb grabbed his laptop and started writing an email to Cooper, the chapter's direct point of contact with the national leadership of IAH. Cooper had just started in his position less than 3 months ago, and this would be the first logistical interaction Kaleb had with him. Despite this, all signs pointed to Cooper being a reasonable person who would be honest with him, and Kaleb felt that this kind of issue is one that he should bring to the attention of his superior for advice. Kaleb opened his email and wrote:

TO: ra5@iah.org

SUB: Policy Question

Brother Cooper—

My name is Kaleb, and I am the president of the Rho Mu chapter of IAH
at Central University. I hope your position is off to a good start. I'm writing
to you with a policy question about one of our probationary members. At
a class meeting the other night, he told a few of us that he was transgender
and that, while he had his name changed with the university and had a
doctor's note, his paperwork wasn't technically complete and wouldn't be
done until late November at the earliest. I saw that, according to the policy,
a person must be both medically and legally male in order to become a
member. Should we go ahead and make him a full member now even
though his paperwork isn't technically done, or wait until the paperwork
comes through?

Fraternally,
Kaleb

Kaleb took a deep breath, hit send, and went to heat up some leftover pizza for
a late dinner. To his surprise, he received an email back within the hour.

TO: kalst@central.edu

SUB: RE: Policy Question

Brother Kaleb—

Thank you for the well wishes! It's been a steep learning curve, to say the
least, but I am eager to get out and meet all of you soon.

Regarding your question, I definitely feel your conflict and empathize
both with you and with the person in question. However, given the policy, the best course of action is for the chapter to rescind the bid for membership until it can be proven that a person is both legally and medically
male. While I understand (and, frankly, would share if in your shoes)
your desire to not wait, it is clear that this disclosure disqualified this
probationary member for the time being, however good his intentions
were. Please do not hesitate to reach out to me if you have any questions
about this.

In Eta,
Cooper
Advisor, Region 5, Iota Alpha Eta Fraternity

Kaleb's heart sank. Even though it wasn't a strong endorsement, a direct authority had confirmed that Kaleb couldn't just let Paul continue the program. This aggravated Kaleb, who knew Paul's heart was in the right place and that the chapter desperately needed him if it wanted to grow. He texted the two other members who were in the room when Paul made his confession: "Can you guys come to my place ASAP to talk about the Paul thing—need to sort this out now."

Within minutes, Jacob and Mason showed up. Jacob, as the brother overseeing the education and membership process, had first-hand experience as to how impressive Paul was as a potential member and leader for the chapter. Mason, as chapter secretary and parliamentarian, was someone Kaleb trusted with rules and fraternal regulations. Between the three of them, they held a lot of the leadership responsibilities for the chapter, especially in the years following the punishment set by the national fraternity.

Kaleb showed Jacob and Mason the policy in the governing documents and the email from Cooper that seemed to seal Paul's fraternal fate. Then, he sighed and asked, dejectedly, "So, I guess we have to let Paul know that he needs to wait until his paperwork clears before he can be initiated?"

Jacob fired back immediately, obviously passionate about the topic. He argued, "Man, that's so stupid. The only reason we're having this discussion is that he felt obligated to tell us something that he clearly didn't want everyone to know. Why should he be excluded just because he was honest?"

"It sucks, but the rules are rules. He's technically not male, so he can't join," Mason said, shrugging his shoulders.

Jacob snapped back, "What do you mean, technically? Do you think he's a man?"

"Yeah, I do," Mason replied, "and I don't have any problem with him. But he doesn't have the ID, so Nationals says he can't join. It's a yes or no question, and right now the answer is no."

Jacob wasn't convinced and turned to Kaleb as if he had an idea. He asked, "Did you tell Cooper you were talking about Paul?"

"No, and it isn't like he knows us yet," Kaleb replied. "He's new, too. What are you hinting at?"

"Well, ultimately, who cares what we do?" said Jacob. "By the time he's a member, Paul will have his ID and no one will care that he didn't have it at the time of initiation."

Sensing Mason starting to push back, Jacob continued to make his case. He argued, "Paul is a man, he's been a man since I've known him, and there's nothing anyone can do or say to convince me otherwise. Besides, what will we tell the rest of the chapter? 'Uh, sorry guys but Paul can't be a member right now because of . . . reasons . . .'"

"Well, we'd just say it, right?" Mason asked. After seeing both Kaleb and Jacob starting to shout him down, he pivoted. "Okay, sorry, not what I meant. But we can say something around it, right? Like that Paul is taking it easy this semester and will be back in the spring to finish up?"

Jacob shook his head. "That won't go over well with his class, who know him well enough to know better."

Mason's voice started to harden. He explained, "Well, what if we bring him through and then someone finds out and narcs on us to Cooper? If it turns out it's not going to finalize for another few months or longer, we're done. We'll have violated policy and initiated someone who was not eligible for membership. We're just now coming off their blacklist; they wouldn't go easy on us."

Kaleb grimaced at the thought of more punishment, but Jacob pushed back, "How the heck would Cooper find out? I met him. He's not the kind of guy who goes snooping around people's private lives like that. There's no way he'd find out."

At this, Kaleb spoke back up with a tinge of spite in his voice. "You really think that if the chapter eventually found out, someone wouldn't be freaked at the idea and report to Cooper that we initiated someone who wasn't a man?" Mason nodded and added, "I can think of a few guys now who would totally do that."

Jacob was visibly disgusted at the thought. "Ugh, really? That's one of the shadiest, worst things you could do to a brother. What you're saying is that we could lose our charter because a brother could become upset that a transgender man is now his brother and whined to Nationals about it, who comes in and finds that a technicality has been not held to 100% accuracy?"

"Exactly, that's how this works," replied Mason. "You break the rules, you get punished. Also, it's just one semester—he'll be back next spring for sure once this gets worked out."

"That's not how this works, though," said Kaleb, pushing back at Mason. "You've seen people give up on the process once they're told they can't join before. We don't know for sure he'd be back in spring, or if he'd even want to be."

"Well, that sucks, but it has to be the case if we want to cover ourselves," Mason answered.

"That's totally against everything we're about, though," said Jason, starting to tear up in his defense. "Paul's already a better brother of IAH than half the guys we have now, and we all know it. Denying him membership on a technicality would go against what we're trying to accomplish. If the rule is bad, I don't care about breaking it if it means the chapter is going to be better for it and someone who deserves membership gets it. Paul belongs in IAH, period."

"I agree," said Mason, the hardness in his voice replaced with a conciliatory tone, "but we can't just throw our chapter away over the status of one person, can we?"

Kaleb sighed and threw his hands up. "All right, it's late. I'm going to sleep on this and figure things out tomorrow. I'll let you guys know what I'm thinking before class, cool?"

Jacob and Mason agreed and all left on good terms, though very conflicted as to what path the chapter should take. Do they follow the policy and temporarily deny Paul membership out of strict adherence to the letter of the organizational policy, or allow a deserving and respected man get what he's earned even if it means violating a clearly defined policy with potentially severe consequences?

DISCUSSION QUESTIONS

1. Which type of organizational leader is best for this situation? Why do you think so?
2. What other types of organizational leadership would work for this organization?
3. How would you approach this decision from a prescriptive model of decision making? Make sure you talk through what each of the steps would look like.
4. Describe this decision-making process from the phase model. What phase are they currently in? What would they then have to do to make a decision?
5. What would you decide to do if you were Kaleb?
6. What other rules might cause a fraternity or other organization to face the dilemmas similar to the ones faced by the characters in this case study?

SUGGESTED READINGS

Canary, H. E., Riforgiate, S. E., & Montoya, Y. J. (2013). The policy communication index: A theoretically based measure of organizational policy communication practices. *Management Communication Quarterly, 27*, 471–502. doi:10.1177/0893318913494116

Meisenbach, R. J. (2006). Habermas's discourse ethical and principle of universalization as a moral framework for organizational communication. *Management Communication Quarterly, 20*, 36–92. doi:10.1177/0893318906288277

18

THE CHURCH MEETING

A GROUP DECISION-MAKING CASE STUDY

Frances L. M. Smith, PhD
Murray State University

Faye walked into the friendly parlor room of her church and chose a seat near the front. The parlor was a room designed to look like a living room, with nice wallpaper, couches, even a chandelier. Other chairs had been brought in for this meeting, as well as a computer and data projector. Slowly, the invited meeting attendees filed in and chose their seats, smiling and engaging in casual discussions as they arrived.

In an attempt to be better organized with regard to the functions of the church, the leaders of the church had been working on a 5-year strategic plan, something Faye knew about all too well having studied organizational communication for several years. Now, the three leaders were ready to reveal their plan to the ministry coordinators, those whose acceptance of the plan would be instrumental to its success when presented to the other 250 church members. The ministry coordinators were each in charge of their own task, and they were all volunteers. There were ministry coordinators in charge of education, senior adult groups, children's ministry, and others. Faye was one of three people leading a ministry for college students, but she was the only one of her ministry represented at this meeting.

This chapter is based on the author's personal experiences.

Faye tried to be optimistic, but her positive self-talk was doing little to squelch her cynicism. Her previous experiences in this organization made her concerned about the leaders' ability to compose a truly strategic and specific 5-year plan that would meet the needs of organizational members. Nevertheless, she arrived at the meeting early, sat near the front of the room, and was ready to participate. She loved this organization; in particular, she loved the ministry she helped to coordinate and she hoped that this 5-year plan was going to be the beginning of the clear vision this church needed so desperately. Until now, most of the work had seemed so unstructured. People's needs were not being met, and she knew it. Others did, too. There had been side conversations among some of the ministry leaders for months regarding the lack of support from the leadership regarding people in various ministries, including Faye's, who needed extra care that volunteers just didn't have the time and resources to provide. When needs aren't met, volunteers leave, members go unserved, and the ultimate goals of the organization aren't reached. Faye felt like she had a crystal ball based on her understanding of organizational communication, and each time she peered into it, she saw the fate of this organization and it looked bleak.

The church leaders entered and opened the discussion with smiles and laughter. They were all older men whose wisdom Faye valued. Although she struggled to understand some of their choices in the past, and she certainly was concerned about the ambiguity in their communication, she wanted the best for this organization, and she knew how important the leaders were to this group. As a volunteer-led organization, everyone in the room (except for the paid ministers) was giving time and effort to make this organization work without monetary compensation. Faye knew this added a whole new layer of commitment and satisficing to the organization's decision-making process.

As the projector warmed up to show the prepared PowerPoint slides, the chairman of the plan spoke, "I have been working together with Evan and Bill to come up with a 5-year plan. Today we'd like to get your thoughts on what we have talked about so far."

Faye was intrigued. *"They want to get our thoughts, huh? Good."* She had been making suggestions for years, but they never seemed to be taken seriously, or at least they were not acted upon. Maybe this is the forum for some change in that regard. Perhaps this plan would reveal to her that they had been listening. After all, she had 7 years of experience participating in and coordinating the ministry for which she was volunteering at this and other churches. It seems as though her experiences in other churches would be valuable to the leadership here.

The chairman continued with his presentation.

"We want to be a family and, as a family, we must consider how we can best work together to create a positive atmosphere of love and care."

Next slide.

"We should work together. Remember, although we are different and we have different talents, we should work together. We should use our talents in ways that benefit one another and the church as a whole."

Next slide.

"We should love one another. Christ teaches us the importance of love. If we are to continue to follow Him, we should be certain that we are showing love to one another and to others."

The slides went on, but the detailed information was absent. How were we to act as a family? How were we to work together? How were we to love one another?

As the chairman continued talking, Faye realized that this was it. This was the "strategic plan." The longer the meeting went, the more Faye saw what was happening and was discouraged. There was no plan here. No clear direction. No real goals. And worse, no reasoning behind what had been "decided."

As the presentation neared its end, the floor opened for questions. A female ministry leader near the front of the room raised her hand and was recognized by the chairman.

"How do I need to prepare my ministry for changes based on this plan?" she asked.

"Certainly, we want to be considerate of how each of you currently operates in your ministries, and we want you to be contributors to the ways this plan will influence your specific ministry activities," replied the chairman.

The questioner smiled and nodded in sincere approval.

Questions were asked and answered with similar ambiguous statements that provided no clear direction but, instead, appeased the solicitor. Faye looked around the room, where 30 people were seated, and noticed no sign of disagreement. No sign of concern. In fact, many people were nodding their heads. Now that the floor was open for questions, people in the room were also having a few small discussions amongst themselves in near-silent whispers.

"This all sounds really great," whispered one older woman seated near Faye.

"Oh yes," responded the man she had whispered to. "It is clear they have been working on this for a long time."

Faye couldn't take it anymore. She raised her hand and was recognized, "I don't understand . . . " Faye began to speak softly. All eyes turned to her, and the whispering stopped. She could feel their cold stares like laser beams boring into the back of her head. Had she really just dared to ask a challenging question? She continued:

"If we are trying to create a plan here, why don't we have a timeline for completion and address some of the serious issues? I know there are people who have unmet needs in this church and they need to be ministered to. We are all trying to work together and do that, but as volunteers, all of us have very limited time and energy to devote to our ministries. I think it would be best if we could hire another paid minister to work full-time and help us take care of these needs."

The chairman looked disgusted that Faye had spoken. How dare she point out a flaw in the "plan." Everyone else in the room remained silent. The chairman said,

"I don't think that is true. Do you all believe that? Are there people here whose needs aren't being met? Do we *really* need to hire someone else?"

A moment of silence passed. To Faye, this felt like an eternity.

"I think this is a great church!" said one man in the back of the room. "I certainly don't think a new hire is necessary."

"Me, too. When I first came here a few months ago, I was so pleased with how everyone talked to me and met my needs. I don't think there is a void," said another ministry coordinator.

Faye was mortified. *"Was no one going to agree with her or at least discuss her viewpoint?"* She knew she was not the only one who saw these needs. She had heard others who were in this room talk about the need to hire someone else in previous conversations outside of this meeting, about whole groups of church members who were not being served, about how the current staff was stretched too thin to handle the load, and how there was only so much volunteers could do. But now all she heard was silence and disregard for her position.

"I think we need to listen to Faye," said one woman who was in charge of the education ministry. "She has been working with her ministry for a long time and she knows what she's talking about."

Silence.

The chairman said something dismissive about the short responses he received and moved on, pretending Faye didn't exist for the rest of the meeting. Her stomach churned. *"How could they not listen to her? How could a room of 30 other people sit in silence or direct opposition to her? Was she the only one who could see a problem with this whole thing? Was she the only one who was willing to have a discussion or voice dissent?"*

Faye appreciated the one person who did speak up, but that person's comment was dismissed as quickly as Faye's. The lack of consideration didn't seem to bother the education ministry coordinator, but it certainly bothered Faye. Sadness, anger, and disgust boiled in her stomach like a hot ball of lava. It was like everything she studied in her organizational communication classes about poor leadership, bad decision making, and groupthink were all happening right in front of her eyes. So many times she had seen the theories and concepts she studied apply to her organizations in a positive way. This was a striking contrast and one that she couldn't seem to combat. *"Was this seriously happening?"* Faye was devastated and infuriated.

She wanted to run out of the room. She wanted to make a scene. She wanted to scream. But she decided against it. She didn't want to show the leaders how upset she was, and she didn't want to compromise her integrity and whatever potential influence she might have remaining by saying something or acting out in a way she might later regret. With great restraint, she kept her mouth shut for the remainder of the meeting and waited to be dismissed. Upon completion of the meeting, Faye started to leave. She noticed her overwhelming feelings had produced a few tears of sadness and anger which had begun to fall down her face. She quickly wiped them away before anyone could see. Under normal circumstances, Faye would have stayed to talk with the other ministry coordinators, her friends. But today, she left and quickly walked to her car.

As she stood by her car, fumbling in her purse for her keys, three other ministry leaders were suddenly by her side.

"Faye, I'm sorry about what happened in there," said Gina, an older woman who coordinated the food ministry. "I know you have a lot of great ideas, but I've been a member of this church for 30 years. You've been here for 3. Trust me, they're never going to listen to you." Faye knew Gina was trying to comfort her, but that comment just made her more depressed and angry.

Wanda, a young woman helping to lead the high school ministry, added, "Yeah, Faye, I wanted to help you out in there, but after I saw how he responded to you . . . well, I mean, uh, you know, I just couldn't bring myself to speak up." Wanda's husband who helped with the high school students and worked with technology for the church was also in the parking lot. "Faye," he said, "I can tell you're upset and I know your suggestions are valid, but maybe the leadership just isn't ready for your ideas. Maybe you just need to let them have more time to think on these things."

By this time, Faye had found her keys and listened to her friends and their attempts at comforting her. It seemed, however, that all that they said just fueled her fire even more. She was resolved to find an answer to what had happened today. She—and others who dared to challenge decision making in future meetings—deserved to be recognized for their ideas and hard work. Now was the time to determine how she was going to proceed. *What was she going to do next?* She didn't exactly know, but she was going to figure it out.

DISCUSSION QUESTIONS

1. What antecedent conditions of groupthink might this group be experiencing? Provide specific examples from the case to support your claims.
2. How is this case an example of faulty group decision making? What are the potential cognitive, psychological, and social influences?
3. How did Faye attempt to manage her emotions during this meeting? What were the organizational expectations for her emotional displays, and how did that influence her display of emotions?
4. What could Faye have done or said differently during the meeting in order to counterbalance the dismissal of the chairman and others?
5. How did the chairman demonstrate characteristics of effective or ineffective supervisor communication?
6. The church is a volunteer-led organization. What role does that context have on the outcome of this meeting? Is the style of leadership affected by the volunteer staff? What other organizations might experience these kinds of problems?

SUGGESTED READINGS

Bisel, R. S., Ford, D. J., & Keyton, J. (2007). Unobtrusive control in a leadership organization: Integrating control and resistance. *Western Journal of Communication, 71*, 136–158. doi:10.1080/10570310701368039

Gallicano, T. D. (2013). Internal conflict management and decision making: A qualitative study of a multitiered grassroots advocacy organization. *Journal of Public Relations Research, 25*, 368–388. doi:10.1080/1062726X.2013.806867

Grant, H. (2014, May). Get your team to do what it says it's going to do. *Harvard Business Review*, 82-87. https://hbr.org/2014/05/get-your-team-to-do-what-it-says-its-going-to-do

Smith, F. L. M., & Dougherty, D. S. (2017). Member-created participatory paradoxes in church decision making. *Southern Communication Journal, 82*, 140–151. doi: 10.1080/1041794X.2017.1315452

ESCALATING CONFLICT AND THE EMOTIONS OF FIRING AN EMPLOYEE

Darius M. Benton, PhD
University of Houston, Downtown

Cynthia L. McCullough, DMin

Lynn, a woman in her mid-30s, was recently appointed CEO of a medium-sized women's clothing manufacture and retail sales company. She spent 5 years with the company, and she completed an MBA and an executive training course offered by the chamber of commerce in her city. Prior to her ascension to this position, Lynn moved through the ranks from middle to senior management and consistently had high marks on her performance reviews. The company, a staple in the community and essential contributor to the local economy, was over 100 years old, and the board of directors placed Lynn in this role upon the retirement of long-time CEO, Mrs. Salley. Upon her appointment, the board directed her to "upfit" the company, increase sagging revenues, revitalize its corporate image, and position the company for survival and growth in the future.

Glenn was an older man, in his early 60s, who had come to the company after being demoted by a competitor. He had a lot of experience and his resume looked good on paper, but he had a reputation for "playing both sides of the fence." Since Lynn's appointment, Glenn had begun to challenge her authority frequently in public and private spaces, even to the point of exhibiting physically combative behaviors.

This chapter is based on consulting and personal experiences.

On one occasion, Lynn was meeting with senior staff to put the finishing touches on a proposed organizational change, which was approved by the board. In usual fashion, Glenn was late to the meeting. He entered loudly, excusing himself and interrupting the meeting's proceedings. When he noticed that Lynn stopped her remarks and waited for him to be seated, he chuckled and gestured toward her, and said, "You may continue."

"No, I'll wait for you," Lynn smiled and replied. She continued, "I was waiting for your report so that we could complete the summary."

"Oh, that," Glenn laughed. "I shot it on up to Dave—thought he should have first crack at it."

"You mean Mr. David Jones, chair of the board, that Dave?"

"Uh, yeah, you know I know him and I know he makes the important decisions. But . . . I'll be glad to send you a copy."

Lynn replied evenly, "You do that." And she finished her meeting without another word to him or comment about him going around her. Glenn, however, had a lot to say about the plans and procedures of other departments, issues outside of his scope, and even wanted to revamp her presentation in several spots. It was difficult for Lynn to keep the meeting on track. Lynn became increasingly concerned since several of her employees also appeared exasperated.

When the meeting was over Lynn approached Glenn, and said, "I don't think you should send reports to the board—that's my job."

Glenn laughed and looked down at her, "Oh Lynn, don't be so sensitive, I was just trying to help you out. It's a big job for a little woman like yourself."

"Not too big. Dave sent the file back to me—unopened—along with a note about controlling my subordinates. Don't do it again." She moved into her office and closed the door, leaving him on the outside.

This was not the first time that Glenn attempted to go over Lynn's head. It appeared that he had an issue with female authority. While the previous CEO was a woman, she was around his age. Glenn kidded and flirted with her to get his way, but these techniques were lost on Lynn. In fact, she had begun not only to distrust his decision making in his own department (his report was riddled with syntactical errors and lacked specificity in several areas) but was also concerned about how he was attempting to make decisions for departments that were not his own. In the past several months, he had become a drain on the system.

He needed to be fired: Lynn knew it; other employees knew it.

After two sleepless nights, wrestling with the dysfunction at the company and particularly ruminating over Glenn's increasing disrespect and overreaching, Lynn called her therapist. She was ambivalent about going to therapy for a work-related issue, but this matter was beginning to damage her personal relationships, disrupt her sleep, affect her mood, and decrease her productivity. "*I hope Dr. Donna can help,*" Lynn thought to herself.

The lunch-time appointment was a welcome change of pace. In contrast to the stressful days of being a CEO, it would be refreshing to have someone like Donna listen to her.

Donna began the first session with "Hello, Lynn, I'm Donna. Tell me what brings you here to therapy today."

Lynn replied, "Hi, Donna, listen, I've got this employee who is driving me crazy. I need for you to tell me how to fire him."

"Relax Lynn. Take a deep breath and let's just get to know each other for a moment."

Lynn countered with "But you see, what I need for you to do is . . ."

"Lynn, relax. Let your shoulders down and breathe."

Lynn interrupted with "What I need is . . .

"Lynn, I sense that you have an issue relinquishing control. Does that feel like something you'd like to explore?"

"Huh? Control? What does that have to do with firing this dumba . . . on my staff? He is undermining the corporate culture, his department is way under its quarterly goals and . . . at the board meetings I'm getting blamed for his shortcomings, *and* he goes over my head to board members and then they snipe at me for not controlling my subordinates! This entire company's success is riding on me! Everything is on me . . ."

"Lynn, who supports you?"

"Huh? What do you mean? I have an executive assistant, an administrative assistant, and 56 other people from marketing folk to custodians who report to me. I don't understand the question."

"You just mentioned 58 people *and* a board of directors who all look to you, who all depend on you, who all have expectations for you. You must be tired of carrying that whole load all by yourself. That's why you came in here and tried to direct this session. You don't expect help, do you? Do you believe that others, especially this Glenn, want you to fail? You are the youngest person to ever hold this position and the company, which was is in rotten shape when you took it over. The board gave you an impossible task and you're doing a terrific job at it—but you must be exhausted."

Lynn looked at the therapist and began to cry. She wasn't sure why she was crying, but when she finished, she felt a whole lot better. She felt as if a weight had been lifted off her shoulders.

* * * * *

At the beginning of their third session, Donna asked, "Well, Lynn, how are you doing?"

"Much better. I've thought a lot about control, about relinquishing some of it, about delegating responsibility—and about not taking Glenn's chiding so personally. Glenn is a troubled man, and I tried to throw him a lifeline by giving him a promotion, but he has abused the privilege and that's not about me—that's about him."

"So are you ready to make him responsible for his own actions and stop carrying his failures on your back?"

Lynn sighed and smiled, "I think so. Glenn's day has come. He's got to go."

* * * * *

When she returned to the office that day, Lynn decided that there was no time like the present to deal with the "Glenn issue." She called him into her office.

"Glenn," she began after he made a great show of sitting and settling himself, "Things aren't going well."

"Yeah, I can see where you're having some trouble. I was thinking . . ."

"No, Glenn, I'm doing fine. The trouble is with your performance. Your reports are always late or sent to the wrong person and often times they lack specificity, vision, or direction for your staff. You refuse to follow the format I developed for weekly reports and that makes things harder for Karen when she's trying to create the summary for me. . . ."

"Well, you see, Lynn, I have my own way of doing those reports; that way you want doesn't suit me. Mrs. Salley had some formats, too, but eventually I got her to see that I could do it may way; you just need to . . ."

"No, Glenn, I don't need to do anything. All of the departments are running well, and making good progress—all except yours . . ."

"Oh, I see. You're threatened by me and my ideas, so you want to get rid of me! Is that it? Well, I'll tell you what! I'll be looking for a new job, and I'll be out of here just as soon as I can!" With that, Glenn exited in an unusually quick fashion.

Yes, Lynn was planning to terminate Glenn in that conversation. She was tired of both his work and his attitude. However, she let that conversation end with his exit as she was not going to play tit-for-tat with a subordinate.

Glenn sulked around the office for the next few days but largely tried to be where Lynn wasn't. His negative talk among the staff increased, and several staff members came to her to complain. When he wasn't second guessing Lynn's decisions to them, he was criticizing their work and attempting to tell them "a better way."

After several days of hearing almost constantly from the staff, Lynn made up her mind that for the sake of the business, Glenn had to go. She caught him in his office and closed the door before he could make an exit. He smiled sheepishly at her.

Lynn began, "Glenn, I need to talk you."

"Uh, yeah, I was going to come to you . . ."

"Glenn, I said I need to talk, and you need to listen." She backed him down into his seat with her hand. "Things are not working out. You are not well suited for this position, and you don't seem happy to be here. I'm sorry, but I have to let you go. We will pay you through the end of the month, but I need you out of here by the end of business tomorrow." With that, Lynn handed him the signed severance letter and strolled out of the room without giving him a chance to reply.

This was Lynn's first position as a CEO. After firing Glenn, Lynn held a meeting with senior staff to answer questions, clarified her actions (within the bounds of employee confidentiality), and restated her confidence and trust in them. As she gained more confidence in herself and allowed those around her to share burdens, employee job satisfaction and profitability increased and Lynn's work-life balance improved, making her a healthier person and a better CEO.

DISCUSSION QUESTIONS

1. What different types of conflicts are present in this story?
2. What different styles of managing conflict are present in the story? Did they seem appropriate?
3. Would a third party have been helpful in navigating this situation? Why or why not?
4. In what ways did bullying, ageism, and/or sexism contribute to conflicts in this case? Consider each character's perspective when answering this question.
5. What positive or healthy outcomes were derivatives of this conflict and ones similar to this scenario?
6. Were the appropriate steps of progressive discipline, including the problem-solving and termination breakpoints, implemented in this case?
7. During the dismissal meeting, what might have been done differently to ensure a smooth exit from the organization?
8. Was Lynn ethically justified in terminating his employment?

SUGGESTED READINGS

Cox, S. A. (1999). Group communication and employee turnover: How coworkers encourage peers to voluntarily exit. *Southern Journal of Communication, 64*, 81–192. doi.org/10.1080/10417949909373133

Cox, S. A., & Kramer, M. W. (1995). Communication during employee dismissals: Social exchange principles and group influences on employee exit. *Management Communication Quarterly, 9*, 156–190. doi.org/10.1177/0893318995009002002

Fairhurst, G. T., Green, S. G., & Snavely, B. K. (1984). Managerial control and discipline: Whips and chains. In R. N. Bostrom & B. H. Westley (Eds.), *Communication yearbook 8* (pp. 558–593). Beverly Hills, CA: Sage.

Gordon, M. E. (2011). The dialectics of the exit interview: A fresh look at conversations about organizational disengagement. *Management Communication Quarterly, 25*, 59–86. doi.org/10.1177/0893318910376914

Kramer, M. W., & Hess, J. A. (2002). Communication rules for the display of emotions in organizational settings. *Management Communication Quarterly, 16*, 66–80. doi.org/10.1177/0893318902161003

Scott, C., & Myers, K. K. (2005). The socialization of emotion: Learning emotion management at the fire station. *Journal of Applied Communication Research, 33*, 67–92. doi:10.1080/0090988042000318521

NEWCOMER SOCIALIZATION AND EXPERIENCES OF SEXUAL HARASSMENT

Andrea L. Meluch, PhD
Indiana University, South Bend

New Employee Orientation

Isabelle was excited to start her first full-time job at TDL Midwest Accounting. She was hired as an entry-level accountant at one of the best accounting firms in the region after graduating from Midwest State University. Isabelle's first week at TDL consisted of an orientation program with the other new hires. The Director of the Human Resources Department, Daphne, led the orientation program.

Over the course of the week-long orientation program, the group learned about TDL's corporate values, the office technology, the organizational hierarchy, and employee vacation and sick time policies. Daphne also described the culture at TDL. She said, "TDL prides itself on having a collaborative environment where everyone works together and looks out for one another. We really are one big family here."

During the orientation, Daphne discussed various policies and procedures employees followed at TDL. Daphne spent the better part of Thursday afternoon going over sexual harassment policies. Daphne played a short video depicting a male manager asking his administrative assistant for sexual acts in exchange for a promotion. After the

---

This case study is based on personal experiences.

video was over, Daphne explained the company policy regarding sexual harassment. She said, "TDL does not allow any sexual harassment in the workplace. We define sexual harassment as any unwanted sexual advances or language of a sexual or obscene nature that makes you uncomfortable."

On the last day of orientation, the new employees discussed what they were most looking forward to in their new positions. When it was Isabelle's turn to share, she said, "I am really looking forward to working with my team and fitting into the family atmosphere at TDL we discussed during orientation."

Meeting the Team

During Isabelle's second week on the job, Carol, her immediate supervisor, worked with her individually and explained specific projects. Carol was very helpful explaining project details and answering all of Isabelle's questions. Carol told her, "I want you to feel comfortable asking me about anything, even if it is not related to these projects. I want you to know that you can come to me with anything, and I am happy to help walk you through it."

Over the course of her second week, Carol introduced Isabelle to the other accountants in her division, Eric, Rhonda, and Richard. Eric was a few years older than Isabelle and had also graduated from Midwest State University. Rhonda had been with the company for 7 years and was about 10 years older than Isabelle. Richard was the most senior person in the division. Although Richard had only been at TDL for 3 years, he had almost 20 years of accounting experience.

On Friday, Carol took the entire team out to lunch to welcome Isabelle into the team officially. Everyone asked Isabelle about her hobbies and favorite television shows. The lunch conversation was casual, and Isabelle liked the camaraderie.

"I just cannot get hooked on *Game of Thrones*!" Rhonda explained when Isabelle shared that it was her favorite show on television.

Richard said, "Well, Rhonda we can't all watch the *Real Housewives of Timbuctoo* all the time. Plus, *Game of Thrones* is great! There's war, dragons, and the female characters are not hard to look at!"

Eric laughed and said, "Yeah, I'm pretty sure it's the best show on television now. I'm so happy Isabelle can join our discussions."

After lunch, the team made their way out of the restaurant and into the parking lot. Carol drove everyone together in her roomy SUV. Isabelle sat in the middle of the backseat in between Richard and Rhonda. After Isabelle put her seatbelt on, she saw Richard looking at her ankle.

"Hey, you have a tattoo on your ankle!" Richard exclaimed.

Isabelle had a small flower tattoo on her right ankle. "Yeah, I got it my junior year of college," Isabelle said.

Richard leaned down and pulled her pant leg up a little to get a better look at the tattoo. "Wow," he said, "I don't think I could ever get one myself. I'm too scared of needles." Isabelle nodded and tried to end the conversation.

"Is everyone buckled up?" Carol asked.

"Not yet," Richard said letting go of Isabelle's pant leg and reaching for his buckle. Isabelle relaxed a little once he let go of her pant leg. She realized how much she had tensed up when he had grabbed her pant leg and was hoping no one else noticed. After lunch, the group went back to the office.

"Adulting Is Hard"

A few weeks later, Isabelle and Eric were walking into the office kitchen to get a cup of coffee. Isabelle started telling Eric about how she was feeling overwhelmed with her upcoming student loan payments and now a new car payment as well. She felt really comfortable with Eric and was starting to see him as a mentor.

"Adulting is hard!" Isabelle joked.

"Yes, and it just keeps getting worse," Eric replied.

Richard then walked into the kitchen and overheard their conversation. "Hey buddy, what's getting worse?" he asked.

"Oh, we are just joking about how hard it is paying off student loans today," Eric said.

Richard perked up and asked, "Do you both have a lot of student loans?"

Isabelle said, "Mine are not too bad, but I just bought a new car to replace the one I used throughout college and my bank account is feeling a little tight. But I feel like that is normal for everyone when they have a new car payment."

Eric nodded in agreement. Richard began pouring himself a cup of coffee. "Well, you know there are more ways to earn money today than just working here," Richard said.

Isabelle was not sure what Richard meant by the comment and felt that the comment seemed a little strange. Eric asked him, "Are you talking about driving for Uber or something?"

Richard laughed a little and said, "Well, for you Uber might be your only option, but Isabelle is a pretty girl. She can earn money in other easier ways if you know what I mean?" Eric shook his head. Isabelle could feel her face getting warm.

Before they could say anything, Richard continued, "There are a lot of places in town that you could get an evening and weekend gig at, Isabelle. With your good looks and the gentlemen's establishments we have around, you could make great money and have those student loans paid off in no time at all if you wanted to."

Eric started to get angry and said, "Richard, that's not cool man. Come on."

Richard looked surprised. "You both know I'm just joking, right?" he said. "You millennials need to learn how to take a joke." He then grabbed his coffee and walked back into the hallway.

Eric asked Isabelle quietly, "Are you okay? I know he meant it as a joke, but it was not funny."

Isabelle just shook her head. "It's fine," she said. "I need to get back to work."

Isabelle walked back to her desk and tried to concentrate on the spreadsheet in front of her, but her mind kept wandering no matter how hard she tried to concentrate. In the moment, Richard's comments did not feel like a joke and it made her feel very uncomfortable, but she was new to the office and did not think it was her place to say something to a more senior member of the staff. Also, Eric said that he knew that Richard was joking, even if he was not funny. Isabelle wondered whether this was normal humor in the office.

Asking for Help

"The numbers are just not making any sense," Isabelle thought as she poured over the document for the third time that morning. Richard had prepared the report, and Carol had assigned Isabelle to review it. Isabelle decided to ask Eric to explain the report to her before passing it along to Carol for final approval.

"Hey, do you have a quick minute?" Isabelle asked, popping her head into Eric's cubicle.

"Of course!" he said turning around. Isabelle stepped into the cubicle.

"So, I've been going over this report for Carol all morning, and I'm having a little trouble with it. Do you think you could go over it with me?"

"Yeah, do you have it up on your computer screen?"

Isabelle nodded, and they walked over to her cubicle. After sitting down, she pointed at the screen and explained her confusion.

"Okay, I see where you are having the problem," Eric said pointing at the screen. He then explained the process for calculating the balances in this type of report. Isabelle asked Eric a couple of additional questions about the process. As they were talking, Richard walked by her cubicle.

"Hey, what are you guys working on?" he asked.

"We're just working on the quarterly report for Smith's Electrics," Eric replied. "But I think we are finished up." Eric stepped out of her cubicle and started walking back toward his desk.

Richard was still standing there and then said, "If you have any trouble with the documents for my clients, you are always welcome to ask me about it."

Isabelle got nervous that she had made a mistake asking Eric for help. She thought everyone in the group was able to help out with each other's clients, but she realized that she had never been told that directly. "Thank you," Isabelle replied. "It was just a quick question, so I grabbed Eric."

Richard then stepped into her cubicle. "You seem so tense," Richard said. He then started massaging her shoulders. Immediately, Isabelle froze up. She was extremely uncomfortable as he lightly rubbed her shoulders.

"Okay, now it's my turn," Richard said with a laugh as he stopped massaging her shoulders.

Isabelle mustered up a sheepish laugh. "I'm not good at massages, and I really need to get this over to Carol before lunch. Thank you and next time I'll be sure to check in with you if I have any questions," she said.

Richard nodded and walked away.

As soon as Richard left her cubicle, Isabelle relaxed. *"How did he think that was appropriate?"* Isabelle thought to herself. She was upset and angry at Richard for making her feel so uncomfortable all the time. Isabelle got up and walked to the restroom to try to compose herself. She closed the bathroom stall door behind her and let out a heavy sigh. Isabelle then heard someone come into the restroom. After a couple of deep breaths, she felt a little better. She opened the stall door and saw Rhonda standing at the sink washing her hands.

"Hey there," Rhonda said looking up into the mirror.

"Hi," Isabelle said walking over to the sink.

"Are you okay?" Rhonda asked. Isabelle realized her face was all red.

Isabelle liked Rhonda but did not know her very well. She was worried if she told Rhonda that everyone would find out what she said and think that she was overreacting, but she was also worried that if she kept quiet she would explode.

"It's just ... Richard kind of rubbed my shoulders, and I felt really weird about it. I don't want to start any problems being new here, but I was really uncomfortable."

Rhonda nodded and paused for a minute. "When did this happen?" she asked.

"Just now," Isabelle said.

"Okay," Rhonda said. "I think you should go talk to Daphne about this. If you felt that uncomfortable, you should talk to HR."

"I'm so new here still. I just don't want to cause any problems," Isabelle said.

"I know and Daphne will know better what to do," Rhonda said.

Rhonda gave Isabelle an understanding glance and then walked out of the restroom. Isabelle continued to think about Rhonda's advice. Isabelle wondered, *"Was it serious enough to go to Daphne? Was this sexual harassment? What if Richard got in trouble? What if everyone thought Isabelle was overreacting?"* Isabelle realized that she was very confused. She felt that she was too new to know what to do.

DISCUSSION QUESTIONS

1. What types of socialization strategies did TDL employ? How effective were these strategies?
2. What information-seeking tactics did Isabelle use to learn about organizational norms? What are the benefits and drawbacks of some of these tactics?
3. In what ways did Isabelle's expectations of her job differ from her actual experiences in the first few weeks?
4. Do you think that Richard sexually harassed Isabelle? Why or why not?

5. At what point should someone exhibiting joking behaviors of a sexual nature be reported to HR or a manager? How could gender differences or generational differences influence perceptions of appropriate joking behavior in the workplace?

6. Do you believe that Rhonda's advice was helpful to Isabelle? Should Rhonda or Eric have taken additional actions to help Isabelle, as a new team member, navigate the situation?

SUGGESTED READINGS

Ashforth, B. E., & Saks, A. M. (1996). Socialization tactics: Longitudinal effects on newcomer adjustment. *Academy of Management Journal, 39*, 149–178.

Bingham, S. G. (1991). Communication strategies for managing sexual harassment in organizations: Understanding message options and their effects. *Journal of Applied Communication Research, 19*, 88–115.

Bingham, S. G. (Ed.). (1994). *Conceptualizing sexual harassment as discursive practice.* Westport, CT: Praeger.

Bullis, C., & Stout, K. R. (2000). Organizational socialization: A feminist standpoint approach. In P. M. Buzzanell (Ed.), *Rethinking organizational & managerial communication from feminist perspectives* (pp. 47–75). Thousand Oaks, CA: Sage.

Dougherty, D. (2000). Women's discursive construction of a sexual harassment paradox. *Qualitative Research Reports, 2*, 6–13.

Dougherty, D. (2001). Sexual harassment as [dys]functional process: A feminist standpoint analysis. *Journal of Applied Communication Research, 29*, 372–402.

Dougherty, D. (2009). Sexual harassment as destructive organizational process. In P. Lutgen-Sandvik & B. Davenport-Sypher (Eds.), *Destructive organizational communication: Processes, consequences, and constructive ways of organizing* (pp. 203–225). New York, NY: Routledge.

Dunn, D., & Cody, M. J. (2000). Account credibility and public image: Excuses, justifications, denials, and sexual harassment. *Communication Monographs, 67*, 372–391.

Keyton, J. (1996). Sexual harassment: A multidisciplinary approach. In B. R. Burleson (Ed.), *Communication yearbook 19* (pp. 93–155). Thousand Oaks, CA: Sage.

Kramer, M. W., & Miller, V. D. (2014). Socialization and assimilation. In L. L. Putnam & D. K. Mumby (Eds.), *The SAGE handbook of organizational communication: Advances in theory, research, and methods* (3rd ed., pp. 525–547). Thousand Oaks, CA: Sage.

THE MORE THINGS CHANGE, THE MORE THEY STAY THE SAME

WHEN INNOVATION MEETS RESISTANCE

Eric D. Waters, PhD
Marquette University

"*Feels like déjà vu,*" William sighed as he reviewed an email forwarded from the corporate headquarters. "*It's gonna be like 2011 all over again.*"

For the past 15 years, William served as regional sales manager (RSM) for the East Texas regional headquarters of Southwest Modifications, Inc. (Southwest Mods), a midsized company that wholesales aftermarket SUV/truck accessories to car dealerships. Since William took over the RSM job, Southwest Mods experienced year-over-year increases in revenue and market share. As RSM, William manages 12 district sales consultants whose territories stretch across Texas, from Dallas to Austin to Houston.

Early on in his tenure at Southwest Mods, William built his sales team with industry veterans he was able to hire away from the major automakers. Guys like Larry, who came over from Nissan, and Marty, who left GM, were in their early 50s when they joined the team. They were old-school, stubborn, and resistant to change, but they were hard workers who knew the business and could hit the ground running. Unfortunately, when the US recession of 2008 hit, William had to let a third of his seasoned team go. Since rebounding from the recession,

---

This chapter is based on the author's personal experiences working in the automotive industry.

William has been forced to grow his team in a more fiscally responsible way, now bringing in talent straight out of college for lower salaries. Young newcomers like Darren and Jose, who joined Southwest Mods in 2013, faced a learning curve with respect to mastering the business and charming dealership personnel. However, both embraced innovation, were authorities on the latest automotive technology, and really shined in explaining the features of the latest dash kits, stereo and lighting systems, and other interior accessories. Larry and Marty often leaned on Darren and Jose for help understanding the more technologically advanced products while offering the pair mentorship and guidance in other aspects of the business.

William just received some news he felt could negatively affect the productivity of his team in the near future. Lynn, the national sales manager of Southwest Mods and William's boss, just sent over the findings of this year's internal communication audit. A communication audit is a means of evaluating information flow in organizations, identifying weaknesses, and recommending changes to address opportunities for improvement. In most cases, an external consulting firm conducts interviews and administers surveys to a company's employees to gain insights on where the company can enhance its communication efforts.

William has been through a few communication audits throughout his career at Southwest Mods, but the last one was less than memorable. Up until 2011, sales operations at Southwest Mods embraced somewhat of a "bring your own device" philosophy. District sales consultants (DSCs) were provided laptops, but allowed to use their own mobile phones to conduct business as they travelled through their respective territories. Every month, the DSCs would simply submit a copy of their phone bill with their other expense reports for reimbursement. However, this policy changed as a result of the 2011 communication audit, which found that DSCs were particularly slow at responding to email. Most of the older DSCs, like Larry and Marty, still used flip-phones with limited data plans. As a result, with virtually no Internet access during an 8-hour day of sales calls, the DSCs would not see their email inboxes until the early evening.

Based on recommendations from the 2011 communication audit results, Southwest Mods began requiring their DSCs to carry company-issued smartphones. The idea behind this change was to make the DSCs more accessible during their workday. With a smartphone, the DSCs could now view and respond to emails during lunch or in between sales calls. Unfortunately, this did not go over well with older DSCs like Larry and Marty, who repeatedly griped to William and other coworkers about having "one more thing to learn" and viewed the smartphone as an "electronic leash." Initially, the two refused to even activate their smartphones in protest. It took nearly 3 months of training, cajoling, and gentle pressure from William to get them into compliance. Even after Larry and Marty started using their smartphones, William had to train them on how to check email from a mobile device and constantly remind them to do so.

Ironically, *this year's* communication audit results found that Southwest Mods *relied too heavily on* email as a means of internal communication.

Employees complained about information overload, citing inboxes of 80+ daily emails. Employees also noted that the sheer volume of emails exchanged made it difficult to locate reports, spreadsheets, and other useful information quickly. Some employees raised the difficulties of collaboration through email alone. Finally, employees also desired the capability to create and exchange more visual messages using graphics, photos, and videos that were standalone, not simply links or email attachments.

As a result of these findings, the consultants who conducted the audit recommended Southwest Mods transition away from email to a single, easily accessible communication interface that supported the exchange of video, photo, instant messaging, and wikis for collaboration. The consultants recommended an "enterprise social media" platform that combined the functionalities of a corporate intranet and a social networking site. William took a deep breath, gathered his thoughts, and called Lynn.

"Hey Lynn, it's William. I just got your email," he said.

"OK. What's up?" Lynn asked.

"Do the suits at corporate know what they are doing to me? What is this enterprise social media crap?"

"William, it's not just about you. These recommendations are for the benefit of the entire company. This is bigger than just the East Texas Region."

"Yeah, I heard that before. Back in 2011."

"Well, it's 2018 now. You have a chance to handle the situation differently."

"How long do I have before we start moving to another system?"

"IT is looking at a platform called Netwrkd. When they clear their recommendation through the CTO, I'll give you a heads-up."

"Yeah, OK. Larry and Marty are going to love this."

Knowing he would have to be creative to sell most of his team on this new system, William decided to do a little research. He found that Netwrkd had several features that addressed the results of the communication audit. In addition to allowing for private messaging between employees, Netwrkd allowed for the creation of groups; the uploading of video, pictures, reports, spreadsheets, and other media; and it had the capability to create and edit documents collaboratively. It could host web conferences for virtual teams and was available in desktop form as well as a mobile app. William also observed that Netwrkd had an interface similar to Facebook. Employees could create posts that would appear in other employees' news feeds, where they could be liked or commented on. Netwrkd would definitely cut down on the need for email, if not eliminate it altogether.

While William was surprised to find some good reasons to adopt the platform, he was more concerned about the cons. For example, what if employees started tuning out during meetings to follow conversations on their mobile devices? Who would manage what type of content was posted? Would this platform exacerbate the spread of rumors or gossip? And most important, how was he going to get Larry, Marty, and the older DSCs to go along with the change?

After a couple weeks passed, William's phone rang. It was Lynn. "William! I just got out of a meeting with the CTO," she announced.

"And?" William inquired.

"You didn't hear it from me, but we're rolling out Netwrkd in about a month. You should get the official notice from IT next week."

"Is IT gonna come train my guys?"

"We've already discussed this. I'm sure you will figure out a way to make this a smooth transition. Do you plan on having your team back in the office anytime soon?"

"We've got a quarterly sales meeting coming up in a couple weeks."

"Sounds like a good time to break the news. Gotta run."

Every quarter, William brought his team in from their respective territories to discuss the past quarter's performance, the upcoming quarter's objectives, and updates from corporate. At 9:00 a.m. on the morning of the quarterly meeting, William gathered everyone in the conference room to kick things off. During the opening session, William congratulated everyone on meeting their objectives, and he identified increases in several key metrics. Next, William rolled out the upcoming quarter's targets and explained the importance of meeting these goals.

After breaking for lunch, William returned to the conference room to begin the closing session of the quarterly meeting. After the team settled in, William began to deliver what he thought might be the most pivotal presentation of the day.

"A couple months ago, we all participated in an internal communication audit," William began. "As always, the objective of these audits is to determine how we can share information more efficiently as a company. When we communicate more effectively, we are more engaged and more productive. As a result of the most recent audit, we will be implementing some changes. Specifically, the consultants suggested that we ease up on email. Too many emails are flying back and forth, filling up inboxes, and burying key information. How many of you can say you are at inbox zero?" No hands went up.

"So, are we supposed to stop using email?" Jose asked.

"Not exactly," William responded. "A better way to put it, we are going to start using what's known as enterprise social media. Corporate has informed me that we will be adopting a platform called Netwrkd. We can post updates, comment, attach files, and exchange messages, just like Facebook. Multiple people can create and edit documents. We will probably use email less and less over time."

Darren nudged Jose and the pair smiled and nodded in approval. Then, as William feared, Larry's hand went up.

"What exactly does this have to do with selling accessories?" Larry inquired. "Why can't I just do my sales calls, hit my numbers, and go home like I have been doing for the past 37 years?"

"Larry, this isn't just about you or me or this team," William explained, recalling that Lynn told him the same thing a little over a month ago. "Decisions like this are meant to benefit the entire company, and we are part of the company."

"Yeah, I remember hearing that when you made us use this," Larry replied, holding up his smartphone. "Now that I finally know what I'm doing with it, you want to change something else! For no good reason!" He then turned to Marty and whispered, "They can't make me use this new networking thing. I won't do it!"

Meanwhile, across the room, Darren and Jose appeared much more receptive to the news. "Does Netwrkd allow us to create and share video?" Darren asked.

"I believe so," William replied.

"What about video-conferencing?" Jose added.

William thought for a minute and nodded.

"Well, I think we should at least give it a try. It sounds like it could make our jobs easier," Darren noted.

"Maybe," Marty interjected, "Or maybe not. Nobody asked us what we thought about Netwrkd. I don't wanna do it. I've got almost 40 years in. Maybe it's time for me to retire."

Just as William feared, at least two of his top DSCs were not taking a company-mandated change well. Lynn told him that this time around, he has an opportunity to handle the situation more effectively. But how?

DISCUSSION QUESTIONS

1. Darren and Jose appear to embrace new ideas, new processes, and new technology. According to the diffusion of innovations theory, what kind of adopters are they? What about Larry and Marty? What role could each potentially play in influencing other DSCs to be willing to adopt Netwrkd?

2. Historically, Southwest Mods has made changes as a result of communication audits. What element of systems theory best represents the cause of the changes? What might happen if Southwest Mods ignored the communication audits?

3. When Larry and Marty grouse to each other and other employees about adapting to organizational change, what type of resistance are they enacting? Discuss the pros and cons of their approach. In 2011, what type of resistance did Larry and Marty display when they refused to activate their smartphones?

4. Despite the advantages of Netwrkd, William worried that the new technology might change his team's interpersonal interactions. Which potential changes resulting from adopting the platform appear to concern William most? What can be done to address these changes?

5. Netwrkd allows for information to be shared and accessed throughout Southwest Mods in several new and different ways. How might using Netwrkd change how Southwest Mods employees establish meaning in their communication? Is this helpful or problematic?

6. During the quarterly meeting, William attempted to persuade his team to accept the move to Netwrkd by stressing its necessity. How did William utilize gain frames and loss frames in his explanation?

7. At the quarterly meeting, Larry and Marty voiced opposition to adopting Net-wrkd. As Netwrkd diffuses across Southwest Mods and alters the communication networks therein, how do you think Larry and Marty's individual roles in those networks might change?

8. Marty hinted at retirement in response to Southwest Mods adopting Netwrkd. How could he have used a more effective strategy to voice upward dissent?

9. The consultants who conducted the communication audit for Southwest Mods suggested an enterprise social media platform would improve collaboration across the company. Determine which primary functions of horizontal communication discussed this might enhance and describe how.

10. As regional sales manager, William exerts influence on the district sales consultants. What type(s) of power does William have over his direct reports? Provide examples of each.

SUGGESTED READINGS

Bertalanffy, L. von (1968). *General system theory: Foundations, development, application.* New York, NY: George Braziller.

Contu, A. (2008). Decaf resistance: On misbehavior, cynicism, and desire in liberal workplaces. *Management Communication Quarterly, 21,* 364–379.

Kassing, J. W. (2011). *Dissent in organizations.* Malden, MA: Polity.

Kassing, J. W. (2005). Speaking up competently: A comparison of perceived competence in upward dissent strategies. *Communication Research Reports, 22,* 227–234.

Lewis, L. K. (2011). *Organizational change: Creating change through strategic communication.* West Sussex, UK: Wiley.

Monge, P. R., & Contractor, N. S. (2003). *Theories of communication networks.* Oxford, UK: University Press.

Rogers, E. M. (2003). *Diffusion of innovation.* New York, NY: The Free Press

Sias, P. M. (2009). *Organizing relationships: Traditional and emerging perspectives on work relationships.* Thousand Oaks, CA: Sage.

Treem, J. W., & Leonardi, P. M. (2012). Social media use in organizations: Exploring the affordances of visibility, editability, persistence, and association. In C. T. Salmon (Ed.), *Communication yearbook 36* (pp. 143–189). New York: Oxford University Press.

22

HOUSE OF PAIN

A CASE OF POWER AND RESISTANCE WITHIN COLLEGIATE FOOTBALL CULTURE

Alaina C. Zanin, PhD
Arizona State University

"Blue, Forty-Two, hut, hut hike!" Chad, a sophomore lineman for Central University, looked up through his facemask as he heard the play called. Chad lunged forward and collided with a lineman from the opposing team. Immediately, Chad felt a sharp pain in his lower back and heard a loud popping sound. The 300-pound defensive lineman he was gripping shoved him to the ground. In a blur, Chad watched helplessly as the defensive linebacker sacked his quarterback. Chad winced and the crowd gasped as the quarterback hit the ground like a rag doll, his head rebounding off the hard AstroTurf. Chad laid on the scratchy plastic grass as his athletic trainer ran on the field. All he could think was, "*Not again.*"

* * * * *

After the game, Chad sat in the Central Eagles' training room holding back tears. This was the beginning of his second year at Central University, and he had finally captured a starting position as an

---

This chapter is based on Zanin, A. C. (2018). Structuring bodywork: Control and agency in athlete injury discourse. *Journal of Applied Communication Research, 46,* 267–290.

offensive lineman for the Eagle's Division I football team. As Chad waited for Frank, the Eagles head athletic trainer, to return with the team doctor, he reflected on how this reoccurring injury would affect his spot on the team and his scholarship.

Chad was an exceptional player in high school and was very close with his teammates and coach. He often referred to his teammates as his brothers and the coaching staff as a family. But since joining the Eagles, he felt more like a number rather than a part of a family. Last year, he sustained a fractured vertebra—an injury that prevented him from participating in most practices and games for his freshman season. He was allowed to "red-shirt" (i.e., not count the season toward his NCAA-allotted four seasons to play a sport) and maintain his full-ride scholarship for his first year with the understanding that he was expected to comply with all the prescribed rehabilitation from the team physician and Frank. This process was time consuming and painful, but Chad attended all 5:00 a.m. and post-practice treatment sessions, doctors' appointments, and complied (mostly) with his at-home rehabilitation exercises. He even set his class schedule in the spring semester to accommodate extra treatment sessions. He had endured needles inserted into his lower back to promote healing. The treatment plan was not a cure-all, but it had helped to reduce his pain. So much so, Frank allowed him to play during the spring scrimmage game. After taking 800 milligrams of Ibuprofen and getting a steroid shot in his lower back, Chad performed well during the game. He continued to improve during this summer's training camp. His increased weight and size due to a coach-prescribed nutrition and strength-training program also helped to make him a top contender for an offensive lineman starting position. His improved performance and strength earned him a starting position on the offensive line for their preseason game.

Laying on the blue vinyl training-room table, Chad saw all his hard work slipping away. As his back throbbed, he tried not to think about the worst-case scenario of having to quit the team and leave the university. Money was tight at home right now, and he knew his parents could not afford tuition and housing costs without his athletic scholarship. Chad glanced over at the training table beside him. His roommate, Sam, a sophomore running back for the Eagles from Chad's hometown, grinned at him. Sam was in the training room because he had been having some pain in his foot, so Frank had held him out of the Eagles first home game.

Sam smiled at Chad and said, "Man, you seriously hurt your back again?! You cannot catch any breaks." He laughed, "Ha, get it? 'breaks.' How long you think you gonna be out? We need you for the regular season, bro." Chad shrugged his shoulders and looked at the ground. Sam tried to cheer him up, "Don't worry, I've got the hook-up for a sweet party tonight and I know there are going to be some fine women there."

Chad rolled his eyes. Sam had never taken football as seriously as he did, even though he played running back since their pee wee football team. It seemed like Sam's talent always made up for not putting in the work in the off-season.

The coaches still put Sam in games as a starter, even though he complained and did not always pay attention at practice.

Frank walked in the room with a frown on his face talking quietly to the team physician, Dr. Harris, and Chad's offensive line coach, Coach Stevens. Chad tried to read their faces, but he could not hear what they were discussing. Frank put his hand on Chad's lower back and said, "Well, the X-rays do not show a fracture, but there is definitely some inflammation. Are you sure you heard a popping sound?"

Chad nodded his head.

Dr. Harris looked skeptically at Chad through his gold-rimmed glasses. "Well, Frank, just keep monitoring his pain; that's all we can go on at this point. There aren't any other standard tests that can tell us when he's ready to return to play. You know what to do for his recovery plan."

Frank nodded, "Yes, I'll definitely keep an eye on him. We know the drill. If we stick to the plan, we'll have him back out on the field in no time. Right, Chad?"

Chad nodded.

Coach Stevens was watching this interaction and said, "You know, Chad, I once broke a bone during a playoff game. Yep, you know I played quarterback back in the day, right? Well, we were all tied-up in the fourth quarter, and I was blindsided. I broke my pinkie, but you know back in those days we didn't have all the fancy medical technology or team physician like you do now. Well, my pinkie was sideways and I just went over to the sideline and had the trainer tape me up. It was my throwing hand, too. I had to play for my team; there was no way I was going to let them down. Well, I completed a 40-yard Hail Mary pass into the end zone to win the game, and we clinched a spot in the championship. You know my pinkie finger still doesn't go straight?" He held his crooked pinkie finger for Chad to see. "But it was definitely worth it."

Chad nodded and said, "I'll do my best, Coach. I'm not going to let the team down again."

Coach Stevens responded, "It's all right son, I know."

✳ ✳ ✳ ✳ ✳

The floor was sticky and the music blared as Sam and Chad made their way into the living room. Sam dragged Chad out to a party at a nearby fraternity house. Sam whistled at a girl, immediately walked over to her, and started dancing. Chad saw some of his other teammates at the party, including the senior quarterback, Chris, who likely suffered a concussion in the game earlier in the day. Chris walked up to Chad and put his hand on his shoulder.

"Hey, Chad, where was Sam today? We really needed him. Didn't Frank hold him out of the game because of a high ankle sprain?" Chris said as he looked over at Sam who was doing some sort of break dance in the middle of the living room floor.

Chad said, "Well . . . uh yeah, that's what Frank said. I'm not really sure what's wrong with him."

Chris replied, "Seems to me like someone needs to suck it up and get back out on the field. You know what they say, 'You can't make the club in the tub.'" Chris slapped Chad on the back, and he recoiled in pain. Chris grinned and said, "Oh yeah, you got pulled into the training room today, too, right after missing a block for me. Jeeze, you sophomores are such wimps. You guys need to toughen up or we're never gonna make it to the championship game."

✷ ✷ ✷ ✷ ✷

Chad arrived in the training room the next Monday morning to check in with Frank. He was not looking forward to the time-consuming process of healing his injury, but he knew Frank would take care of him. Frank's office door was closed, but he could hear the voices of Frank, Head Coach Haines, and Chris inside. Chris was saying, "You know they're not telling the truth when they're out at the Kappa Phi house on game day doing keg stands and dancing with sorority girls. It's total bullshit."

Coach Haines responded, "If someone is hurt and they claim they can't practice due to an injury, fine. But you never really know if a player is really hurt as bad as he says he is. So we're gonna have exercises for '*injured*' players to do during practice. I'll bet you'll find out, *it's amazing*, some guys will heal a lot quicker by having to be over there. We can call it 'The House of Pain.'" Chad heard laughter from inside the office, and the door opened.

Frank walked out and saw Chad. He said, "Hey, Chad, you're here for your rehab? I think that today we will have you go out onto the field with the strength coach. We're gonna have you do a modified workout so you don't lose all your strength."

Coach Haines added, "Yep, son, we have a new policy: Everyone attends practice, even if you're injured, to do a modified workout. Because we need to make sure that you're prepared to contribute to the team when you return to play. I mean, we need to make sure you're earning that scholarship of yours. No free rides on this team."

Chad nodded and went out to the football field to find the strength coach. For the next 2 hours, Chad found out that the "House of Pain" lived up to its name. He completed hundreds of sit-ups, push-ups, burpees, and body squats on the sidelines in full view of his teammates as they ran plays. There was a heat advisory for the day. Chad felt light headed, but he did not dare ask for water. Chad knew most of his teammates and the coaches thought he was faking his injury. The strength coach told him to stop the workout if he was in pain, but Chad knew that the team would think he was more of a wimp if he could not complete the workout in the "House of Pain." Even though many of the exercises hurt his back, Chad clenched his teeth and continued the workout. Finally, the strength coach told him to hit the showers. Chad walked behind the bleachers and vomited. He made the decision to get off the injured list as soon as possible; anything was better than the "House of Pain."

* * * * *

Tuesday morning Chad went into the training room to find Frank. The previous evening he searched the Internet for his injury symptoms. He thought he might have a bulging disk in his back, but he knew he had to convince Frank that he was fine. Since the X-ray did not show a broken bone, all Chad had to do was get Frank to believe he was pain-free. Before entering the training room, he had taken some Vicodin he had left over from getting his wisdom teeth removed. The medicine curbed the pain and he knew he could at least get through practice. Frank came over to the table Chad was laying on.

"So how'd we do yesterday and last night? It seemed like you were okay in the strength workout or did you have some pain?" Frank asked.

Chad nodded and responded, "Yep, I think I'm on the mend. I really feel much better after these few days off. I think I'm ready to get back out on the field. My pain is honestly a two on a scale of one to ten."

Frank eyed Chad, "Hmm, well that seems odd because on Saturday you said it was a nine. Are you sure you're feeling that much better?" Frank put his hand on Chad's lower back and studied his face.

Chad tried to mask the expression of pain on his face. "Yes. See, that doesn't even hurt," Chad lied.

Frank looked at Chad skeptically and said, "Okay, Chad, I'm going to trust you, but please be careful today. We don't want to reinjure it. You could do serious damage if you aren't careful. Remember you only have one body, so treat it with respect."

Chad nodded and got up off the table. "I know. I will."

Chad smiled as he walked into the locker room. His plan worked! Now none of his teammates would make fun of him for being a wimp. He could reclaim his starting position, he wouldn't have to suffer through another "House of Pain" workout, and he wouldn't have to show up for treatment at 5 a.m. Chad laced up his cleats, rubbed some Icy-Hot on his back, and swallowed one more painkiller for good measure. Finally, he was in control of his injury.

DISCUSSION QUESTIONS

1. In the end of the case, how can you tell if Chad was resisting or complying with organizational norms and values?
2. How are aspects of the organizational culture (e.g., stories, assumptions, mantras, norms, and values) influencing athletic health and injury reporting?

3. What strategies do organizational members in this case use to pressure Chad to follow team norms?
4. In what ways does Chad demonstrate power and control in this case?
5. In what ways are power holders in the organization regulating Chad's behavior? Provide examples of surface-level uses of power as well as uses of deep power structures.
6. How might deep power structures, like the ones in this case, be present in other types of organizations?
7. Should organizations regulate, surveil, and dictate worker health care and wellness practices? Does the type of work or profession influence these practices? Why or why not?

SUGGESTED READINGS

James, E. P., & Zoller, H. M. (2018). Resistance training: (Re)shaping extreme forms of workplace health promotion. *Management Communication Quarterly, 32,* 60–89.

Zanin, A. C. (2018). Structuring bodywork: Control and agency in athlete injury discourse. *Journal of Applied Communication Research, 46,* 267–290.

Zoller, H. M. (2003). Health on the line: Identity and disciplinary control in employee occupational health and safety discourse. *Journal of Applied Communication Research, 31,* 118–139.

Zoller, H. M. (2014). Power and resistance in organizational communication. In L. L. Putnam & D. K. Mumby (Eds.), *The Sage handbook of organizational communication* (pp. 595–617). Thousand Oaks, CA: Sage.

VOLUNTEER MANAGEMENT, ROLE EXPECTATIONS, AND (DIS)EMPOWERMENT

Lacy G. McNamee, PhD
Baylor University

Helena Grider had been actively involved in Refuge, a center for homeless youth in downtown Houston, since its founding. Its mission of providing a safe space for teens to eat, shower, and do homework after school was especially meaningful to her given her decades as a school guidance counselor and her experiences working with kids who didn't have a stable guardian or place that they considered home. After retiring several years ago, she started spending more and more time at Refuge each week, mentoring, helping with meals, office work, cleaning—really anything that she could do to help.

Today, as she addressed envelopes for a year-end mailer to donors and other constituents, she silently contemplated the conversation going on between Refuge Executive Director Elise Howard and Case Manager Victor Martín just a few feet away.

"So, what do you think?" Elise asked Victor. "Do we just skip the holiday party for the kids this year? Attendance was lousy last year. Honestly, it's just starting to feel like a bust."

This chapter is based on ongoing field research, personal experiences, and consulting.

"Yeah, I know," replied Victor. "But I hate to cancel it altogether. I get your point, though. It's never really been the feel-good event for them that I think we envisioned it to be."

"Exactly. Still, I'm torn." She stared silently for a minute and then turned. "What do you think, Helena?"

"What?" Helena was caught off guard. Even though she was accustomed to the staff discussing work in her presence, she wasn't used to being pulled into the conversation.

"Yeah, you're with the kids all the time. You probably know them better than we do," Elise said, encouraging Helena to join the discussion.

"Uh, well, I know money is tight, and we don't want to spend a bunch without anyone showing up, but . . . " Helena paused, at first, but then decided to say what had been running through her mind all along as she listened on. "What about redirecting those dollars to gifts that we could surprise them with when they drop in? We could try to think of something useful and specifically meaningful for each kid. It wouldn't have the communal aspect of a party, but I think it would make them feel connected to us and this place."

Almost without hesitation, Elise exclaimed, "That's perfect! Let's do it."

Victor echoed, "I like it. Great idea."

Helena was surprised but thrilled by their reactions.

That night, Helena retold the conversation and her idea to her husband, Robert, over dinner. She realized how good it felt to have her voice heard and respected, almost as if she was one of the staff. After dinner, she received a text from Victor asking if she could come in the next morning to "chat and get the ball rolling" on the gift list. She quickly replied, "Yep!" and began brainstorming ideas.

* * * * *

The next morning, Helena pulled up to the parking lot at Refuge right as it opened.

"Thank you for coming in so early, Helena," said Victor as he invited her into the office. "So what if you take the first stab at coming up with gift ideas for each of them while I'm in a meeting? Then I will circle back with you in about an hour or so. Sound good?"

"Sure, sounds great," said Helena.

Victor motioned toward his desk as he headed toward the door. "Okay, great. Make yourself at home as always. I'll see you in a bit."

Helena settled into Victor's desk chair, grabbed a legal pad and pen from the drawer, and began to write. Her ideas came quickly as she pictured each teen's unique story, personality, and needs. Before she realized it, an hour passed and Victor was back.

"So, whatcha got?" smiled Victor, as she handed him the pad. He browsed through the list for a minute and then said, "Looks great, but what's this?" Victor pointed to the bottom of the sheet where it said "TBD drop-ins."

Helena had jotted down some gift ideas for kids who might be new to Refuge or sporadically appear around the holidays. Helena answered, "You know, we always get a few newbies around that time. I figured we want them to be included, right? So those are some things that might appeal broadly to different people." It seemed obvious to her. Still, she sensed some confusion on his end. Or was it something else?

"I mean, I guess," Victor replied slowly, "but don't you think we can just get those gifts if and when that situation arises? Or even just wait and give them a gift later after the holidays if they keep coming more consistently? I just don't think Elise is going to want to spend money unless it's on one of our regulars."

Helena, surprised and a little ruffled by Victor's reaction, sat silently for a moment. Eventually, she responded: "Yes, but doesn't that come off as kind of exclusionary? These kids have experienced enough rejection and abandonment in their lives, haven't they?" She didn't mean for her words to come off harshly, but she knew the emotion had come through in her tone.

After a few moments of seemingly tense silence, Victor managed a hollow, "Uh, okay. We'll see." With that, the conversation abruptly ended as he politely excused himself to a "lunch thing."

* * * * *

"Can you believe that?" Helena exclaimed to Robert when she got home. "I mean, he asked for my opinion, but then he didn't even respect it! He himself admitted that I probably know more than he does."

Helena had stewed about her conversation with Victor as the day wore on, so by 6:00 p.m. her husband received the brunt of her pent-up frustration. Typical of his analytical and diplomatic self, Robert attempted to ask probing questions yet reserve judgment.

"So, forgive me for potentially asking a dumb question, but what's so bad about waiting to do those gifts at a later time? It's not like he was saying that they didn't deserve gifts, just that you might hold off, right?"

Helena snapped back, "Yeah, but you just can't do that. Look, I know these kids—not just from Refuge, but from years and years of working with them in the school system. Even the slightest rejection has a huge impact. They don't process it the way you and I do."

Realizing she was nearly shouting at Robert by now, she paused, took a deep breath, and then continued with a softened voice. "Look, I'm sorry I got so worked up." She sighed. "It's just a really big deal."

"I don't doubt it," Robert responded and patted her on the shoulder. "Just give it a day or two and then readdress it with Victor. I'm sure he'll be willing to listen."

She forced a smile. "Yeah, you're right. I guess I owe him that."

That night, Helena tossed and turned in bed, replaying her conversations with Victor and Robert over and over again in her head. Perhaps exhaustion was to blame, but as she lay awake in bed, a nagging question eventually settled in her mind: *"Why should I have to be the bigger person? I'm just a volunteer."*

* * * * *

The next morning, Helena woke feeling calmer about the gift situation but also a little guilty about her mounting negativity toward the Refuge leadership in general. She mulled over her conflicted thoughts and emotions: She loved the Refuge mission and her time with the teens, yet she was frustrated and feeling taken for granted. *"Am I just their little reliable and compliant 'worker bee?'"* she wondered. Feeling no resolve, she decided to take a long jog and try to clear her mind.

When she returned, she showered and prepared to run a few errands before some afternoon appointments. As she grabbed her phone on the way out the door, she noticed a missed call and voicemail from Victor. *"Great,"* she thought begrudgingly. *"What's he want now?"* Feeling the anger from the night before start to creep back in, she hit play:

"Hey, Helena, it's Victor. Look, I just wanted to follow up after yesterday and say, well, first of all, that I'm thankful for you for all you do and . . . " he paused. "I'm sorry if I didn't react well to some of your ideas. I actually ran the fallback gift idea past Elise, and she totally agreed with you. So, yeah. Thanks again for always going the extra mile, and . . . maybe just call me when you get this."

She was taken aback by his heartfelt message. She listened to it once more, feeling a strange mix of relief and shame. On one hand, she felt vindicated: *"Of course, Elise agreed with me. I was right!"* she thought. At the same time, she was embarrassed that she had become so frustrated and bitter. Just as she was about to dial him back, she decided to drop by Refuge instead to clear the air. It was on the way to the store, so she jumped in the car and headed toward the center.

As she walked through the door, she stopped to chat with two of her favorite kids. Stella and Darian were both close to finishing high school and working hard to start trade school next fall—a huge victory considering that Stella was close to juvenile detention a few months ago and Darian had been in and out of five schools in less than 2 years.

Elise appeared in the doorway from the next room, smiling at the group. "Hey, Helena, so good to see you. I didn't realize you were coming in today?"

"Oh, well, I'm not really," Helena replied. "I was just coming by to touch base with Victor. Is he here?"

"Actually, he just stepped out, but I'm glad you're here. Before you go, stop by my office. There's something I wanted to run by you." With that, Elise grabbed a cup of coffee from the kitchen and disappeared back into the office suite.

Helena followed a few minutes later. She settled into the cushioned armchair in Elise's office expecting to talk about the holiday gift list. "Helena, I hope you know how much we value you," Elise started. "Honestly, I can't imagine this place without you—not just your time, but your heart and vision for this place. Just like with the gifts. You know our kids so well, but you also know what we need as an organization. I have no idea why I haven't thought of this before, but would you be willing to serve on our board of directors?"

Before Helena could process the unexpected turn in the conversation and respond, Elise continued. "I know it's a lot to think about. It's more time, of course, but it's also time well spent. You know this, but we're a small board, and I view our board as an extension of myself. Every major decision we make as Refuge, it's not just me. It's six people making those decisions with me, thinking through the financial, logistical, short-term, and long-term implications. To be honest, we've asked some of our volunteers to be on the board before, and it's been a disaster. Sometimes the passion for the kids gets in the way of making big-picture decisions for the agency as a whole, but I think you're different. You can shoulder the responsibility, and we need your voice and contribution. What do you say?"

"*Whoa*," thought Helena. This was not at all what she was expecting, and her mind raced with questions: *Isn't this what she had been wanting—a more respected voice and position? At the same time, isn't retirement supposed to be about less responsibility, not more?* She was a little dazed and struggled for what to say.

"Um, wow, Elise. This is not what I was expecting." She paused, trying to make sure that she responded appropriately. Elise's words had made her feel validated and overwhelmed all at the same time. "Don't get me wrong, I'm flattered. I mean, thank you for thinking of me . . . but can I think about it?"

Elise, somewhat confused and subdued, replied, "Uh, of course. Take your time."

After a few moments of awkward silence, they exchanged pleasantries and promises to touch base again in a few days. Elise then accompanied Helena out of the office suite and returned to her desk, puzzled. As she sank into her chair, she wondered where her intuition had failed. She was certain Helena would be thrilled to join the board. Had she read her all wrong?

DISCUSSION QUESTIONS

1. What are Helena's motivations for volunteering at Refuge? Were Victor and Elise responsive to these motivations?

2. To what extent did Victor's and Elise's management approaches differ? What is the best type of management approach for a volunteer like Helena?

3. In what ways did Victor's managerial approach impact Helena's life outside of Refuge?

4. To what extent is Victor or Elise responsible for how volunteers' experiences at Refuge overflow into other parts of their lives (e.g., family, work)?

5. What elements of surface and deep structure power are evident at Refuge? How do these power dynamics encourage or stifle volunteers like Helena to speak up to the leadership?

SUGGESTED READINGS

Ashcraft, K. L., & Kedrowicz, A. (2002). Self-direction or social support? Nonprofit empowerment and the tacit employment contract of organizational communication studies. *Communication Monographs, 69,* 88–110. doi:10.1080/03637750216538

Clary, E. G., Snyder, M., Ridge, R. D., Copeland, J., Stukas, A. A., Haugen, J., & Miene, P. (1998). Understanding and assessing the motivations of volunteers: A functional approach. *Journal of Personality and Social Psychology, 74,* 1516–1530. doi:10.1037/0022-3514.74.6.1516

Garner, J. T., & Garner, L. T. (2011). Volunteering an opinion: Organizational voice and volunteer retention in nonprofit organizations. *Nonprofit and Voluntary Sector Quarterly, 40*(5), 813–828. doi:10.1177/0899764010366181

McAllum, K. (2014). Meanings of organizational volunteering: Diverse volunteer pathways. *Management Communication Quarterly, 28,* 84–110. doi:10.1177/0893318913517237

McNamee, L. G., & Peterson, B. L. (2014). Reconciling "third space/place" toward a complementary dialectical understanding of volunteer management. *Management Communication Quarterly, 28,* 214–243.

BALANCING ON A TIGHTROPE

MAKING WORK-LIFE DECISIONS
IN DUAL-CAREER COUPLES

Sarah E. Riforgiate, PhD
University of Wisconsin, Milwaukee

Rebekah Carnes, MA
Kansas State University

Miriam waited until she was alone to look at the email again. She opened her laptop and stared at the glowing screen, slowly reading the job description one more time. She couldn't believe it was such a perfect fit. Just thinking that she had options made her excited, but she had not mentioned the job to anyone because she wasn't sure she wanted to apply.

Things hadn't been ideal at work. With the reorganization, it seemed like every day was longer than the one before—an uphill battle, full of frustrations. Despite Miriam's experience and expertise, she didn't feel valued. Projects she had spearheaded were set aside for other organizational agendas. She and her coworkers were frustrated with new policies and procedures. Miriam, one of the few women in her department, spent much of her days listening to her coworkers complain, trying to calm people down, absorbing others' frustration, and redirecting the negative energy to positive tasks. She felt honored that people trusted her, but it was exhausting to navigate the emotional waters at work.

This case study is based on a combination of interviews from several published work-life studies.

Spending so much time encouraging others, she fell behind on her own work and compensated by working longer days and taking work home. One silver lining was the work flexibility she had. With three children, it was great to be able to work at home when they were sick or rearrange her schedule to get to doctor appointments and school events. She knew not all employers would allow her so much flexibility. Still, she worked 60 or more hours a week and checked emails constantly. She considered transferring divisions, but there weren't any openings that fit her skills.

She thought, "*I don't want to go on the job market again. I know the ropes. I have a nice office and lots of vacation time. I am vested in the retirement program. I don't want to move.*"

Yet there it was on the screen—an ideal job posting forwarded from a friend who thought she "might be interested."

Miriam was interested, but changing jobs would mean moving her whole family to a new state. She cringed as she thought of packing up their house and starting over; moving seemed like too much to even consider. Finding doctors, changing addresses, learning a new town, figuring out a school system . . . the challenges seemed to go on forever. She reflected on the obstacles, "*The kids won't want to leave their friends. Eric would have to find a new job. It just doesn't make sense to apply.*" She reasoned, "*Even if I do go through the hassle of applying, they might not offer me a job or enough money to make it worth the move.*" Miriam tagged the email and closed her laptop for the evening. She would sleep on it and broach the topic with her husband, Eric, later.

Saturday morning Miriam woke as the soft morning sun flooded through the windows. She went downstairs and sat next to Eric with a cup of steaming coffee in hand. She loved the quiet calm Saturday mornings allowed. It was the best time to reconnect with Eric after a hectic week. Miriam had considered the position for a week, but kept the information to herself until she was ready to talk about it. After exchanging good mornings and discussing plans for the day, it seemed like as good a time as any to ask Eric what he thought.

"Eric, an interesting email came across my computer about a week ago."

"Really? What was it about?"

"Well, there is a position in Montana that seems like it was written for me, and I haven't seen another opening at this company for several years. It would be a dream job, but I doubt they would hire me."

"Miriam, why do you say things like that? Of course they would hire you. Tell me about the position." Eric never understood why Miriam always downplayed her talents.

Miriam explained that the position was specific to what she had been doing for the past 15 years and that there were not many people certified in her industry.

"Honey, you should apply!"

"No, I don't think I will. It's just nice to know there is demand out there for my skills."

"Really, you should apply. Worse case, they don't offer you the job. Best case, they do and you can make the decision to go or not."

Miriam objected, "What about your job? What about the children? The thought of even *considering* moving makes my stomach turn. Besides, I should focus on making my job better, not changing jobs. People are counting on me."

Eric encouraged, "The way I see it, you have nothing to lose here! Besides, how long can brushing up your resume and filling out an online application really take? You should go for it!"

Miriam let a smile stretch across her face, "I love you, Eric. Thank you for being so supportive. I will give it some more thought."

Miriam appreciated his support, but it wasn't that easy. This wasn't just about her and the job. Eric seemed to miss that it was about *all* of the family and the obstacles that came with starting new lives for five people.

Eric couldn't understand why Miriam just didn't apply. It would be a great move for her and help her get out of her comfort zone. She could make new connections and grow professionally. Lately, she wasn't excited about her current job. In fact, some days she was miserable. She was putting in long days and came home frustrated, complaining about the new direction the company was taking. Eric always listened, but there wasn't much he could say or do that would change things. Miriam spent a lot of time worrying about her coworkers' problems, too, which was difficult for her.

This position would offer Miriam a fresh start, which would be good for her. Eric wanted her to be happy. Miriam put so much time and effort into her career and loved what she did, just not always where she worked. She probably wouldn't move anyway, but it would be good for her to feel wanted and valued.

After many conversations and Eric's encouragement, Miriam lined up reference letters, filled out the online application, double-checked her documents, and held her breath as she clicked "submit." It was out of her hands now.

Three weeks passed and she hadn't heard anything. Miriam conceded, "*I should just make the most of where I am.*"

She told Eric, "It just wasn't meant to be. Besides, it is so much easier to stay, and I don't want to disrupt you and the children. In the end, it is probably better that I wasn't tempted with an offer."

Eric replied, "You know how slow these processes are. They will call you."

Indeed, they did call. The next thing Miriam knew, she was flying out for the interview and they offered her the job by mid-November. "*Now what?*" she thought. Things were picking up for Eric at his work. The children were settled in school and almost halfway through the school year. Moving would be hard on everyone. She felt a knot growing in her stomach and rather than feeling elated, she was distraught.

She had a week to answer—yes or no? The new company wanted Miriam to start right away, offering her the chance to lead her own project, hire two additional team members, an additional $10,000 in annual salary with stock options and a signing bonus, and relocation expenses. Miriam's mind raced with a jolt of adrenaline. She thought about the possibilities of a fantastic new position. "*This is the chance to have coworkers and a team who actually like where they work*," she thought. When she started at her current job, she had felt the expectation to maintain harmony and to take care of everyone, but her coworkers seemed stuck in a negative cycle that she couldn't change, which drained her energy. She daydreamed, "*Starting in a new company with contented coworkers would free me to focus on my own work. I would have time to be innovative and creative with autonomy over my own projects. How can I say no?*"

But then she thought, "*How can I say yes? Even if this is a great opportunity, it is terrifying to change jobs. This isn't just about me. How can Eric and I make it work? Will the children hate me for moving them away from their friends in the middle of the school year?*" She tried to figure out if it was possible to commute three states away for the rest of the year. Her mind raced as she worked through concerns. "*How many of the children's activities would I miss? Would Eric be able to get all three of the children to school, practices, and activities by himself during the week? Who would attend parent–teacher conferences? A new position would mean less work flexibility— I don't want to give that up. I would have to start my vacation accrual clock over again, making summers difficult with the kids.*"

Miriam also worried about what this new job would mean for Eric. She remembered a party they attended, where one wife commented to the husband of another saying, "Oh, I have never met a trailing husband before!" Miriam knew it would be harder on Eric to move for her career than the other way around. She sighed as she thought, "*People don't know how to respond to successful women. Is it worth putting Eric through the awkwardness of explaining to family and even perfect strangers that he is following my career? What if he doesn't find another job right away? Will Eric be happy staying home and taking care of the children after school?*"

Miriam told herself, "*I should be happy. I have a good job and the possibility of another great job. This is a win-win proposition, right?*" But she felt like she was balancing on a tightrope—no matter what move she made next, she was going to fall and disappoint someone. She sighed and lamented, "*There is no way to make everyone happy.*"

When Miriam told Eric she received a job offer, Eric smiled broadly and congratulated her with a warm hug. He encouraged, "If this is what you want and it will make you happy, you should take it! We can figure the rest out."

Eric really did want Miriam to be happy. She had been so miserable at work, she hadn't been sleeping well, she had been short with the kids lately, and she rarely smiled. She complained about work for so long that Eric was motivated to see her happy again, free of the stresses that occupied her mind and their conversations.

Eric continued, "My career field is much more flexible. I am sure there will be plenty of positions wherever we move. The children will make new friends and this might even be a chance for us to all grow closer together. Miriam, this is a great offer! You should accept. What are you waiting for?"

Privately though, Eric did have some doubts. This move would bring a lot of change. He would need to develop a new network. He remembered Miriam staying home with the children when they were younger and complaining that people at parties would ask, "So what do you do?" and then make patronizing comments about how hard it must be to stay home to raise children. She noted that her parent identity was less valued than a worker identity. It was more typical for mothers to stay home with young children. Eric worried, "*Will people be critical of a stay-at-home father? Will I be all right in between positions while I am not working? How will I explain this to Mom and Dad?*" He wasn't sure his parents, or her parents for that matter, would understand. Eric pushed the questions aside, figuring things would work out. Nevertheless, some doubts lingered.

DISCUSSION QUESTIONS

1. Dual-earner spouses face dilemmas about which career to follow. Considering this case study, should Eric or Miriam's career take preference and why?
2. How do Miriam and Eric experience social expectations to adhere to motherhood norms, ideal worker norms, individualism norms, and consumerism norms? Considering messages you have been exposed to in your family, schooling, and through the media, which norms and identities are privileged over others in society, and how does this influence communication about work and family?
3. Which of the work-life policies and practices are important factors for Miriam staying or leaving her current position? If Miriam pursues this offer, what should she negotiate for with her future employer? Since women and men are perceived differently when they negotiate, what communication framing should Miriam use that might be different from framing Eric would use?
4. What other work-life conflicts do dual-earner couples face? How do organizational policies and workplace communication shape these conflicts?
5. Is work-life conflict an individual, organizational, or societal issue, and what are the ethical implications for each orientation?
6. As Miriam and Eric navigate work-life boundaries in their respective career trajectories, they use multiple strategies to mitigate the stress that work-life conflict can cause in overall satisfaction with life. How does their decision making reflect boundary management strategies (high segmenting to high integrating) with a decision that will affect both public work and private life spheres?

SUGGESTED READINGS

Babcock, L., & Laschever, S. (2003). *Women don't ask: Negotiation and the gender divide*. Princeton, NJ: Princeton University Press.

Bowles, H. R., Babcock, L., & Lai, L. (2007). Social incentives for sex differences in the propensity to initiate negotiation: Sometimes it does hurt to ask. *Organizational and Behavior and Human Decision, 103*, 84–103. doi:10.1016/j.obhdp.2006.09.01

Buzzanell, P. M., Meisenbach, R., Remke, R., Liu, M., Bowers, V., & Conn, C. (2005). The good working mother: Managerial women's sensemaking and feelings about work-family issues. *Communication Studies, 56,* 261–285. doi:10.1080/10510970500181389

Denker, K. J., & Dougherty, D. (2013). Corporate colonization of couples' work-life negotiations: Rationalization, emotion management and silencing conflict. *Journal of Family Communication, 13,* 242–262. doi:10.1080/15267431.2013.796946

Kirby, E. L. (2017). Work-life balance. In C. R. Scott & L. K. Lewis (Eds.), *International encyclopedia of organizational communication* (pp. 1-21). Chichester, UK: Wiley-Blackwell. doi:10.1002/9781118955567.wbieoc068

Kirby, E. L., Riforgiate, S. E., Anderson, I. K., Lahman, M. P., & Lietzenmayer, A. M. (2016). Working mothers as "jugglers": A critical look at popular work-family balance films. *Journal of Family Communication, 16,* 76–93. doi:10.1080/15267431.2015.1111216

Medved, C. E. (2016). Stay-at-home fathering as a feminist opportunity: Perpetuating, resisting and transforming gender relations of caring and earning. *Journal of Family Communication, 16,* 16–31. doi:10.1080/15267431.2015.1112800

Riforgiate, S. E., & Boren, J. P. (2015). Communicating domestic labor task resistance and equity restoring strategies among married individuals. *Journal of Family Communication, 15,* 309-329. doi:10.1080/15267431.2015.1076421

NEW BEGINNINGS, NEW CHALLENGES WHEN GLOBAL AND LOCAL COMMUNITIES MEET

Kathleen J. Krone, PhD
University of Nebraska, Lincoln

Chigozirim Utah Sodeke, PhD
Eastern Illinois University

On the surface, Mid-City USA was a stereotypical Midwestern city: politically conservative, racially homogenous, and agricultural. By the mid-2000s, however, Mid-City had settled refugees from 56 different countries. Refugee resettlement was now a part of Mid-City's story and identity. In many ways, it was a planned change that involved deliberate action from local and federal agencies. For instance, Lutheran Family Services (LFS) and Catholic Social Services (CSS) were primarily responsible for welcoming refugees to Mid-City and received a one-time sum of $1,875 per refugee from the US Department of State to help newcomers navigate their first few months in the United States. Refugee resettlement required a complex set of health, legal, employment, social, and educational services, as well as resources that extended beyond these first few months and beyond the capacity of any single organization to provide. In reality, refugee resettlement also created a host of unplanned changes in the community that must be addressed.

This case study is based on observations of task force meetings, interviews with task force members, and personal experience.

To address these changes, the New Beginnings Task Force (NBTF), a loosely connected network of governmental and community-based, nonprofit organizations, was formed. During NBTF's monthly meetings, police officers, immigration lawyers, public school administrators, social workers, employment agency staff, city administrators, health care workers, and other organizational representatives gathered to share information and resources, talk about their problems and triumphs, build collaborations, and evaluate the progress of programs and initiatives designed to meet refugee needs.

Over the years, NBTF operated as an organic system, learning and growing in response to their work with new arrivals. Member organizations came from an active and thriving, frequently faith-based, nonprofit community and learned to work well within a politically conservative and religious state—a state that boasts one of the highest rates of volunteerism in the United States (www.nemosaic.org). Vibrant, nonprofit involvement was vital for meeting needs that government and business organizations were unable to meet (Frumkin, 2005). NBTF members recognized the need to interact with these macro forces actively and with Mid-City's shifting demographic and cultural environment in order to identify and make necessary multilevel adjustments in response to changes in the community.

NBTF as a community-based partnership was not unique. Interorganizational partnerships often are formed to address social, economic, and political challenges in communities (Heath, 2007). But it is difficult work filled with uncertainty. NBTF Board Chair Jean, and Board Members Mariana, Raymond, Noah, and Matthew met on a regular basis to talk over some of their most pressing challenges.

* * * * *

It has been another hectic day at Mid-City's Human Services Office. Jean rubbed her aching head and poured another large cup of coffee. She was used to complex cases, but preparing Mid-City and its organizations for the growing refugee population has been draining. She checked her watch; 15 minutes to spare before the next NBTF board meeting. She quickly glanced at her notes and walked down the hall to the meeting room. To her surprise, Mariana, Noah, Matthew, and Raymond were already seated. She masked her exhaustion and gave them a cheery smile.

"Wow, you guys are early," she said.

"Yeah, Jean. We are feverish with energy and excitement," replied Matthew. Everyone laughed at his sarcasm.

"Calm down, Matthew." Jean joked. "Do you guys want to go ahead and get started early?" Everyone nodded eagerly.

"Awesome!" continued Jean. "Okay . . . let's see what we have here. So, I received a request from one of the departments at the university. They are planning a cultural fair and would like us to suggest some refugee families that they could feature during the show."

Raymond snorted, struggling to control his distaste. "Give me a break," he complained. "I've been to one of those so-called 'cultural fairs' and all they do is parade people around like cultural specimens. They are human beings, for crying out loud!"

The others nodded in agreement. Jean rubbed her throbbing head again.

"So, what do you want me to tell them?" Jean asked. "I mean, I get what you are saying, but we need these kinds of partnerships with the university."

"Well," Noah said, "you could refer them to the Mosaic Project website. The School of Journalism has been developing that for years and they do a really good job of featuring refugee stories and experiences."

"Good point. You know, it wouldn't hurt for these departments to start talking to one another," Jean argued.

Matthew chimed in: "I agree. The university could provide a little more leadership along these lines. When I talk with members of different departments, they often have good ideas, but they don't seem to have any idea that other departments are doing similar things."

Jean said, "Right, yes, well let's move on. I would like us to talk about what's happening in the schools. I bumped into an acquaintance of mine the other day, Mary Beth Wheeler. She's the principal at Douglas Elementary and they are doing a lot of exciting things. Mariana, she said you were collaborating with them on a new initiative."

"Yes," replied Mariana, "I was waiting for today's meeting to update everyone. Douglas Elementary is working with Lutheran Family Services for our annual block party. This time, we are going to have games, snacks, and street food from different countries represented at Douglas, and the kids and their parents get to participate. The children are so excited."

"That sounds great, Mariana," said Noah.

"I can't wait to see it all come together. It was hard moving to Lincoln myself, as an adult refugee. I cannot imagine what it feels like as a child. These kinds of events can really make you feel like you belong in the community, you know," she added.

Matthew offered, "Well, let us know if Catholic Social Services can do anything to help."

Mariana thanked Matthew and added, "Sometimes I think I may have bitten off a little more than I can chew. I do want to discuss something, and I promise I'm not trying to be negative."

"Go ahead, Mariana," Jean offered encouragingly.

Mariana began, "The social side of things is just as important as the education, and I think many teachers are only focused on the educational part . . . English as a Second Language and that sort of thing. But we are not thinking enough about how children can have a very different experience based on what 'type' of refugee they are."

The others looked curious. Puzzled, Matthew asked, "What do you mean 'type'?"

Mariana continued, "Okay, for instance, one complaint I hear is that the darker-skinned kids are often ostracized."

"You mean the African kids?" Jean asked.

"No, not just them," explained Mariana. "Refugee kids in general who have skin on the darker end of the spectrum tend to have a harder time. Some Sudanese friends with very dark skin have had repeated issues with other children calling their daughter an 'African booty-scratcher.' It's almost like a darker complexion is more easily associated with foreign-ness—and that is undesirable."

"So, colorism basically," Noah offered sympathetically.

"Exactly," Mariana responded, "and it's not just the kids. It can also be hard for darker adults to get jobs. It's one of those things that is talked about within the refugee community, but the larger community needs to be educated about these less-discussed prejudices."

Matthew added, "I'm glad you bring this up, Mariana, because I think sometimes when we throw around the 'diversity' word, we oversimplify what's really going on here . . . you know, everyday life stuff. For example, another problem I've been hearing about are the bus routes. There just aren't enough to get people from point A to point B. No matter how willing you are to work, if you can't get there, what are you going to do?"

"Yeah," Noah nodded supportively. "The practical things are so crucial, like being able to get recertified in the United States. I meet refugees all the time who are skilled doctors, lawyers, accountants and yet they work in meat-packing plants because the recertification process is so long and difficult. I think it creates the impression that all refugees are good for is low-wage, low-skill jobs."

"Yes, and those stereotypes are the hardest things to shake," added Matthew. "I don't even mention the word 'diversity' anymore when I'm talking to local businesses."

Everyone chuckled, knowingly.

Raymond sighed and added, "Oh, it's like a curse word."

"Clearly, we have a lot of work to do in preparing the community practically *and* mentally for the people that are arriving here," argued Noah, "and we have to be real about what is happening and what we are seeing."

"That is a great segue to our next agenda item," Jean asserted. "As you all know, with Noah's help, we have developed two short films featuring METCO's commitment to hiring refugees and I'd like to get your feedback on how effective the films have been in encouraging other businesses to hire refugees."

Noah added, "As you know, the first video featured the personal story of METCO's CEO, and it has created some buzz. Some people are really inspired by this man's commitment to hiring refugees."

"But let's be real, though," interjected Matthew. "Is this guy's personal story representative of the CEOs of most big companies in the city? You can't count on most of them to do the right thing. Most of these guys are more interested in the bottom line than they are in doing something for someone else."

Noah frowned and added, "Well, what about the second video that features a METCO supervisor and one of his employees, a former refugee? Remember, this is the one where the supervisor enthusiastically endorses the work ethic of this employee and praises him for always smiling and being happy at work."

Raymond snorted again. Jean began to feel herself getting tense.

Struggling to control himself, Raymond said, "Okay, Noah, you know I have a lot of respect for what you do, but jeez Louise! What was all that stuff about how the refugee was always so 'happy' and 'grateful' for every American crumb. I mean, when you listen to the part where the refugee is allowed to speak for himself, he sounds just like any other American worker."

Noah looked a little offended. Seeing Noah's face, Mariana jumped in. "I think what Raymond is trying to say is that there might be more value in hearing *more* refugee perspectives."

"Hey man, I'm sorry if I came off wrong," added Raymond. "I'm just concerned, you know. Social media is everything these days, and this sort of thing really affects how the community looks at people. All I'm saying is that the supervisor's condescension was kind of off-putting. I mean, who does the guy think he is?"

There was an awkward silence. Jean's head was throbbing so hard she can barely concentrate.

To close the meeting she said, "So it has been a long day. I suggest we continue this discussion during our next meeting. I will forward you a copy of the agenda."

Without speaking, everyone packed up their things, and the board meeting adjourned.

DISCUSSION QUESTIONS

1. Reflect on Raymond's irritation about the cultural fair. How do organizations display and use diversity in problematic and exploitative ways?
2. Discussions of diversity can be very emotional. How can organizational members navigate and manage these emotions in productive ways?
3. Do you disagree with Raymond's open and unapologetic display of emotion? Why or why not?
4. What are some common conflicts that conversations around diversity produce?
5. Why do you think the idea of "diversity" doesn't appeal to Mid-City employers? Do you have any ideas for how to handle their resistance?

6. How might members of the NBTF better prepare their community for under-standing the changing demographics of the workplace in Mid-City?

7. Has your community or organization experienced a significant cultural change? How did they respond?

SUGGESTED READINGS

Frumkin, P. (2005). *On being nonprofit: A conceptual and policy primer.* Cambridge, MA: Harvard University Press.

Heath, R. G. (2007). Rethinking community collaboration through a dialogic lens: Creativity, democracy and diversity in community organizing. *Management Communication Quarterly, 21,* 145–171.

Norwood, K. J. (2015). "If you is white, you's alright...." Stories about colorism in America. *Washington University Global Studies Law Review, 14,* 585–607.

GOSSIP, A LEADER'S COWARDICE, AND A GLASS CEILING EXPERIENCE

26

Deanna L. Bisel, *BBA*

Ryan S. Bisel, PhD
University of Oklahoma

It was 8:05 a.m. Dee had just arrived at work and J. T., her boss, called. "Dee, I need to see you in the conference room at 9." Early morning meetings were not unusual, but his tone was stern and angry. As she hung up the phone, Dee noticed two employees passed by her office window. They seemed to glare at her, which was unusual.

"*Must be a situation in one of the plants we need to discuss,*" she thought to herself.

J. T. was executive vice president of Operations and had been Dee's boss for 5 years. Dee was promoted from being a general manager of a small town manufacturing plant to an executive position at headquarters in the city. Everyone told her it was a huge deal to be a female executive in the largely male-dominated multinational organization, Card Collections. And that's the way she felt: She was on her way up.

The conference room was located between Dee and J. T.'s offices, so they used it often. As she walked to the room, Dee could feel her staff watching.

"We need to talk about your performance," J. T. said.

This chapter is based on personal experiences.

Dee was surprised as performance reviews were not supposed to occur for another 3 months. J. T. continued, "I think it is time for you to return to one of the manufacturing plants and one of the production services positions."

Blood drained from Dee's face. This would be a demotion. "But I had my performance review a few months ago, and I got a very good rating. Can you be specific about my performance?" she asked, shakily.

"I'm getting tired of your obsession about recommending women for promotions," he responded flatly. His eyes looked unusually distant for the man Dee came to consider her mentor and friend.

She was stunned. After a breathless pause, Dee said, "But when you promoted me to this job, you told me that you wanted me to be the person who made sure there were always women on the list of candidates when we have management openings. I'm confused."

"Start thinking about what plant you want to work in, and Harry Crane will handle the details." With that, J. T. walked out.

Dee stumbled back to her office and closed the door. She had just sat down when the phone rang.

"I want to see you, immediately," Harry said on the other end of the phone.

As if in a fog, Dee made it down the three flights of stairs to Harry's office. Harry was the vice president of Human Resources at Card Collections for the Operations Division. Harry and Dee were old friends and their families did things socially. They worked together for 10 years in the same production plant, and both of them had been moved to Corporate about the same time. Dee hoped Harry would straighten this out for her. Instead, he was cold and strictly business.

"Dee, I know this may have caught you off guard, but it is for the best. You need to think about what plant you want to work in and whose production services position you want." He spoke at Dee like a stranger and not as a friend. He avoided eye contact. It was like everyone's nonverbals changed overnight.

"But, Harry, all the guys who hold those jobs are my friends. I can't do that to any of them." Dee felt light-headed.

As if prepared for the comment, Harry said quickly, "You have a few weeks to think about it and then we will make the decision for you if you can't."

Fighting back tears, Dee started for the door and went for a walk around the parking lot to gain some composure. She kept asking herself, *"What happened? How did I get here?"*

* * * * *

After completing college, Dee landed a job with the phone company, and her parents were delighted. In her small town, jobs with the phone company, railroad, or government were highly prized. On the first day of her first "real job," Dee's supervisor walked her to the mail room and presented her with a mail cart—it was a scene out of a B-rated movie. After 2 years of pushing the mail cart, she went to her supervisor and asked for a new position or she would be leaving.

His replied, "Nobody leaves the phone company."

Three days later, Dee gave her notice.

Dee found a job as an intern for a local printing company, and they promised to teach her the business. She fell in love with the graphics business. Some years later, she was introduced to Bill Wilson, a plant human resource manager for Card Collections. Bill recruited her, saying that the company was interested in hiring more minorities and female managers. Dee was offered a job as a supervisor in one of their small offices of five women. She accepted the job. Dee gave birth to her second child after 3 years with Card Collections. When she returned from 6 weeks of maternity leave, her career started moving faster. She was promoted to department manager with a department of 80 women. One year later, Dee was promoted to production control manager and became the first woman to hold a top plant position in the company's history. Her team was responsible for scheduling all the production through the plant, the warehousing operations, and the computer hardware and software.

Dee's boss, Larry Moore, mentored her.

Larry said, "Dee, I am determined to coach you to become the first woman in our division of 6,000 people to make it to senior management."

Dee felt that Larry's management style was like a head coach. Every encounter with him was a learning experience.

When Larry was later promoted, he recommended Dee for his old position. So she became the first female in the Operations Division to become a production manager. Dee oversaw seven department managers, who were each male. Additionally, she oversaw 70 supervisors and 600 production employees.

The day after Dee took the position, one of the male department managers asked to see her. "My wife is upset that I will be reporting to a woman and told me to come in today and quit," he said.

Dee responded, "But you have over 25 years with the company, but, if that is how you feel, we will miss you."

He stayed.

Dee got the call to headquarters after she worked for Card Collections for 10 years. J. T. called and asked to see her. To her delight, J. T. wanted to promote Dee and pay for her family to move.

They both knew the importance of the situation: Dee would be the first and highest ranked woman in the Operations Division—a position one level below the senior executive team.

"We need your help," J. T. said in a friendly but serious way. "One of the reasons you were offered this job is that we need your help in promoting other women. I need for you to make sure when we have management openings that there is always at least one woman on the list."

Dee was thrilled! Her family loved the new home, schools, and neighborhood. The job was everything she dreamed of, and she got to help other women while doing it. Now, 5 years after being promoted, that dream was crumbling. What could have gone wrong?

Just last month, J. T., six other direct reports (all male), and Dee had an offsite retreat. At the retreat, Dee presented a solution to a major short-term staffing problem. J. T. and her peers complimented Dee, and that evening they all went out for dinner, drinks, and a few laughs. J. T. even toasted Dee for the new idea.

"Here! Here!" and "Cheers!" still rang in her ears.

*****

Then, it occurred to Dee.

She spoke with J. T. the night before he demanded her transfer and demotion. "Hey Dee, where you heading?" called J. T., from his car window. He was driving out of the parking garage and Dee was walking along the sidewalk.

"My daughter had a dental appointment this morning, so I came in late and had to park in a garage two blocks down the street."

"Hop in and I will take you," he replied. He reached over and opened the passenger side door of his luxury car.

Dee got in and thanked him. Dee directed him to the distant parking garage where she parked earlier. The pair passed a few employees who were walking to their cars and she waved. One gave them a strange look.

An empty parking spot next to Dee's car made it easy to idle and chat. The pair had not seen each other that day and so, like normal, they discussed several pressing business issues. The two waved at a few more employees as they got in their cars. More strange looks were sent their way. About 20 minutes later, J. T. and Dee said goodbye. The next morning would be a completely different story.

DISCUSSION QUESTIONS

1. Dee's demotion and transfer were unexpected, which triggered her sensemaking. Employees were apparently also engaged in sensemaking, after they saw Dee and J. T. together outside of work. What does that indicate about the power of informal communication networks and sensemaking?

2. How would you characterize the leader-member exchange (LMX) quality between J. T. and Dee in the weeks and months preceding her demotion? How might their LMX quality have shaped Dee's sensemaking or shaped other employees' sensemaking?

3. Why might J. T. have decided to demote and transfer Dee as opposed to terminating her employment altogether?

4. What messages might the presence of women in top-level management positions send to other women within a company? Send to men within a company? Send to external stakeholders? What messages might Dee's demotion send?

5. What is the ethical implication of delegating the responsibility to include women candidates in hiring pools to a woman employee? Whose responsibility should it be?

6. What is the role of moral courage in withstanding the ill effects of gossip? What kinds of gossip are likely detrimental to increasing workplace diversity and diversity in management generally?

SUPPLEMENTAL READINGS

Buzzanell, P. M. (1995). Reframing the glass ceiling as a socially constructed process: Implications for understanding and change. *Communication Monographs, 62,* 327–354.

Elsesser, K., & Peplau, L. A. (2006). The glass partition: Obstacles to cross-sex friendships at work. *Human Relations, 59,* 1077–1100.

Hafen, S. (2004). Organizational gossip: A revolving door of regulation and resistance. *Southern Journal of Communication, 69,* 223–240.

Kurland, N. B., & Pelled, L. H. (2000). Passing the word: Toward a model of gossip and power in the workplace. *Academy of Management Review, 25,* 428–438.

(IN)VOLUNTARY ORGANIZATIONAL EXIT AMID CHANGE, CONFLICT, AND RESISTANCE

Anne Kerber, PhD
Minnesota State University, Mankato

Marya Wilson, PhD
University of Wisconsin, Stout

Cathy took a deep breath before she opened the doors to the Human Resources office. "Hi there," she said as she smiled at the receptionist, trying to appear calm despite the butterflies in her stomach. "I have a 9:15 with Tricia. I know I'm early."

"Perfect. I will let her know you're here," said the receptionist as she returned Cathy's smile.

Reflections on a 20-Year Career

As Cathy settled into a lobby chair, she thought about her career leading up to her exit interview. She started working at Eastlake Hospital (EH) more than 22 years ago as a nurse and patient educator. After 2 years, Cathy was offered the opportunity to fill in temporarily as a medical communication specialist, writing material to market EH's clinical services to outside physicians. She couldn't have imagined she would still be doing this work 20 years later. Yet Cathy relished the challenges of blending creative writing with her medical

This chapter is based on in-depth interviews with 15 professional women, as well as our own experiences in industry.

background. Cathy also enjoyed mentoring her younger colleagues, most of whom were in their 20s and 30s. "They keep me young," she joked when she told stories about peers seeking her advice on writing, balancing work and family, and navigating EH's internal politics.

She loved her job. Rather, she *had* loved her job until EH hired Dr. Theresa Jefferson, a new president and chief medical officer, and Susan Miller, a new director of marketing and communications. Cathy heard Dr. Jefferson was a transformational leader who would radically reshape EH's culture. But she never actually seemed to be at EH and was always traveling to fundraise for the hospital. Susan was responsible for implementing her strategic vision during these absences. Cathy wasn't sure about the new leaders' ideas. In her opinion, EH was already doing many things well. Why change it?

Going in a New Direction

"The draft of the e-newsletter is good, Cathy, but it just seems too . . . Hmm." Susan drummed her fingers impatiently as she inspected the document. "I guess, there's too much doctor-speak." She sounded annoyed. "I mean, most newsletters wouldn't include footnotes."

"Of course." Cathy felt defensive. "But this newsletter goes to our physician network. We know this specific audience wants to hear medical jargon. It tells them we speak their language." Susan still looked doubtful. "The footnote? Doctors love factoids and evidence. We would never use it with any other audience."

"That might be what EH did in the past." Susan folded her arms. "But Dr. Jefferson is looking for a more streamlined approach to marketing. Fewer specialized audiences. More return on the investment from each of our communications. And that means all of our writing needs to be translated into clear, ordinary English."

"I don't mean to overstep, but is that a good idea?" Cathy asked. "If we use everyday language with the doctors, they'll dismiss it as just marketing and won't read it! We're in a competitive market for clinical services, and we rely on the physician network for referrals. Is this a risk we can afford to take?"

Susan snapped abruptly, "I appreciate your questions, but we don't have time for second-guessing, Cathy. This is what Dr. Jefferson wants. And we need to do our jobs. So I want you to rewrite this and get it back to me by tomorrow morning." She looked pointedly at Cathy. "Are we clear?"

"Crystal clear. I'll get right on it." Cathy shuffled her papers together and fled Susan's office.

"*It's fine. You're fine*," Cathy repeated to herself, trying to soothe her shock and frustration, as she walked back to her cubicle. "*She's new and stressed out—which makes sense; she's got a lot of responsibilities. You'll figure her out. And you can give this new style of writing a whirl. It's not like you're the curmudgeon who says, 'We've always done things this way.' This old dog still knows how to learn new tricks.*"

The Frustration Builds

"Knock, knock!" Cathy heard Dr. Dan Schmidt's booming voice behind her. Swiveling her office chair, she smiled, "It's nice to see you, Dr. Schmidt. What brings you over from pediatrics?"

"Always a pleasure, Cathy," Dr. Schmidt returned her smile. "Say, what's the status of our e-newsletter? I reviewed a draft that looked like it was ready to go, but that was, what, 3 weeks ago? Our team is hoping to get it out as soon as possible."

"I'm so sorry about the delay," Cathy grimaced. "With the leadership changes, our approval process is taking much longer than normal. Susan is making sure it aligns with Dr. Jefferson's new messaging strategy."

"Great." Dr. Schmidt rolled his eyes. "Well, I'm sure they'll get right on it."

"They will," Cathy promised, sensing Dr. Schmidt's displeasure. "The biggest challenge with any new marketing strategy is ensuring you have the right messages for your audiences. It isn't an easy thing! I'm meeting with her tomorrow, and I'll put it at the top of our agenda."

"Thanks, Cathy," Dr. Schmidt said and smiled. "And, we—I mean, me and the other docs—understand you're not the problem here. We've counted on you to do great work for longer than I can remember. It's just frustrating things are getting hung up when we've already given them the green light. I heard the internal medicine mailer took almost 6 months to get out, and we can't afford that kind of delay."

"I hear you," Cathy said. "And, I will talk to her about it tomorrow."

Stuck in the Middle and Struggling to Adapt

A year later, Cathy walked down the hall to her weekly meeting with Susan, her stomach tight with anticipation. Although she worked hard to integrate the more casual language that Susan and Dr. Jefferson wanted into her writing assignments, Cathy was still struggling to get the doctors to buy into the new approach.

"That sounds stupid," one doctor had said, pointing to Susan's requested edits. "We don't say it that way. I won't sign off on this." Cathy understood their frustration. She still thought the new leadership team was underestimating the importance of the doctors' voices.

Making matters worse, EH's marketing analytics were starting to reflect Cathy's biggest fear: Readership and click-through rates of the physician e-newsletters had dropped by 7% in the last 6 months. Cathy tried sharing the data with Susan, but she seemed too invested in Dr. Jefferson's vision to worry about the decline. It was no wonder Cathy was experiencing more headaches and insomnia. Her job stress was at an all-time high.

"Hi. Are you ready for me?" Cathy smiled as she arrived at Susan's office.

"Hey Cathy, have a seat. I was just looking over your latest revisions on the women's health team brochure," Susan replied. Cathy's heart sank as she saw the red editing marks covering the paper.

"I think you're getting closer to matching the new voice for our communications," Susan said. "But we're not quite there. I'm still seeing too much medical-speak here. Can you tweak this section so it sounds more down-to-earth? And I want to see some wording and punctuation changes there."

"I hear what you're saying, Susan, I really do." Cathy could feel her frustration rising already. "But it was like pulling teeth to get Dr. Reed and her colleagues to approve this version. They just don't believe other doctors will pay attention if we simplify the language any further."

Susan frowned. "But, Cathy, that's on you. We are developing a unified voice for EH, and you need to sell the doctors on the new strategy. You're a good writer and clearly understand what they want to say. All you have to do is package the language in ways that would be more accessible to a general audience, even if it's just the docs who are going to be reading it."

"Look. I know we've gone round and round on this, Susan." Cathy struggled to find the right words to mask her exasperation. "But doctors want evidence! I don't know how to sell them on a strategy that our numbers don't support. If anything, last quarter's analytics proved they're right. Our audience engagement with physicians is down—not a lot, but enough to take seriously. Don't you think this merits recalibrating our strategy, especially before it has the potential to impact EH's bottom line?"

"We've talked about this—at length, I might add," Susan scolded. "There are a number of other important variables impacting the data. But you also don't shift a long-term marketing plan for short-term results. I'm starting to think you're struggling to sell the strategy to physicians because you don't buy into it yourself. I sincerely hope that's not the case. But if you aren't fully committed to Dr. Jefferson's vision, perhaps your talents would be better utilized somewhere else."

Cathy was speechless. She desperately wanted to defend her concerns as evidence of her commitment to EH. But she didn't want to antagonize Susan any further.

"You know that I'm a team player, Susan," she said pointedly. "Let's just move on. I've tried to rewrite this brochure three different ways. Clearly, I'm not getting it, and I don't want to waste any more time. Can we work through this trouble section together?"

Staying or Going?

"It's good to be home," Cathy said as she put her purse on the entryway table and kicked off her shoes.

"Hey! How was your day?" Her husband, Joe, greeted her with a hug. Cathy could barely grumble a response. "Ooh. That good, huh?"

"I just can't seem to get through to Susan," Cathy sighed. "She wants me to completely redo the women's health brochure. Again. For the fourth time! 'Make it simpler, more accessible,' she says."

"Yikes!" Joe said. "What will Dr. Reed say?"

"What do you think?" Cathy glared at him. "She was furious about the last round of changes!" She paused. "Sorry. Some days, I think this job is going to be the end of me. And it's just so sad. It used to be great. But Susan doesn't respect my knowledge or experience."

Joe looked at her thoughtfully. "Why don't you quit? Or at least retire early. "

"What?" Cathy was stunned. "But we were planning to wait a couple more years!"

"It would be earlier than expected, but let's take a look at our finances," he reasoned. "You're so unhappy at work. Let me ask you this: Do you think the situation will get better in the next couple of years?"

"It doesn't look good," Cathy fumed. "But who hires an almost 60-year-old these days? And what would I even do with myself if I retired now?"

"Have some fun, for a change," Joe teased. "You don't have to quit working entirely, either. Remember the freelance writing opportunity for Westwood Health Insurance a while back? Maybe that's another possibility."

"That's not a bad idea," Cathy mused. "A couple of my former interns are in the marketing department over at State Hospital now, too. Maybe they could use a part-timer. I'll see if I can set up a lunch date with them."

The Exit Interview

"Cathy?" Tricia appeared suddenly. "It's nice to see you again! Why don't we talk here," she gestured to a conference room down the hallway.

"We really hate to see you go. You've had such an excellent record here. 22 years!" Tricia smiled as she closed the door and both women sat down. "But I understand why you wouldn't want to pass on the opportunity to retire early. That's exciting! As you know, we conduct exit interviews with all departing employees in order to improve our workplace culture continuously. Can you tell me how your job matched your expectations?"

"Yes," Cathy said, "But just so you know—this isn't only about me wanting to retire early. I mean, that's not exactly the whole story."

"Oh?" Tricia's eyes widened, surprised. She picked up a pen and leaned forward, "Please tell me more."

Cathy paused. "*How much should I actually tell her?*" she wondered, "*Will it even make a difference at this point?*"

DISCUSSION QUESTIONS

1. Would you categorize Cathy's decision to retire early as the result of a shock, gradual disenchantment, or a mix of reasons? How do such factors complicate the characterization of organizational departures as voluntary, involuntary, or the third form of exit (that blurs the distinction between voluntary and involuntary)?

2. Put yourself in Cathy's shoes. How much information would you share with Tricia about your reasons for leaving? Under what circumstances do exit interviews enable or constrain the disclosure of valuable information?

3. What are some ethical implications that emerge from exit interviews? For instance, what are some of the potential risks (for the interviewee or their former colleagues) of disclosing a principled rationale for departure? What obligations are created for the interviewer by exit interview disclosures?

4. Based on the story, how would you categorize Cathy's conflict style? Susan's conflict style? In what ways might supervisor-subordinate differences in managing conflict disrupt their short-term and long-term working relationship?

5. Organizational change sparks resistance frequently. How might leaders benefit from listening to upward dissent, such as the concerns raised by Cathy and the physicians? What are the potential costs of ignoring or silencing members' resistance?

SUGGESTED READINGS

Anderson, L. B., & Jiankun Guo, S. (2018). The changing face of retirement: Exploring retirees' communicative construction of tensions through bridge employment. *Communication Studies, 69*, 196–212. doi:10.1080/10510974.2018.1437056

Avery, C. M., & Jablin, F. M. (1988). Retirement preparation programs and organizational communication. *Communication Education, 37*, 68–80. doi:10.1080/03634528809378704

Cox, S. A. (1999). Group communication and employee turnover: How coworkers encourage peers to voluntarily exit. *Southern Communication Journal, 64*, 181–192. doi:10.1080/10417949909373133

Gordon, M. E. (2011). The dialectics of the exit interview: A fresh look at conversations about organizational disengagement. *Management Communication Quarterly, 25*, 59–86. doi:10.1177/0893318910376914.

Hewlett, S., Luce, C., Shiller, P., & Southwell, S. (2005). *The hidden brain drain: Off-ramps and on-ramps in women's careers.* Center for Work-Life Policy/Harvard Business Review Research Report, Product no. 9491. Cambridge, MA: Harvard Business School Publishing Corporation.

Hirschman, A. O. (1970). *Exit, voice, and loyalty: Responses to decline in firms, organizations, and states.* Cambridge, MA: Harvard University Press.

Jablin, F. M. (2001). Organizational entry, assimilation, and disengagement/exit. In F. M. Jablin & L. L. Putnam (Eds.), *The new handbook of organizational communication: Advances in theory, research and methods* (pp. 732–818). Thousand Oaks, CA: Sage.

Klatzke, S. R. (2008). *Communication and sensemaking during the exit phase of socialization* (Unpublished doctoral dissertation). University of Missouri, Columbia, MO.

Klatzke, S. R. (2016). I quit! The process of announcing voluntary organizational exit. *Qualitative Research Reports in Communication, 17*, 44–51. doi:10.1080/17459435.2015.1088894

Kramer, M. W. (2010). *Organizational socialization: Joining and leaving organizations.* Cambridge, UK: Polity Press.

Smith, F. L. M., & Dougherty, D. S. (2012). Revealing a master narrative: Discourses of retirement throughout the working life cycle. *Management Communication Quarterly, 26*, 453–478. doi:10.1177/0893318912438687

APPENDIX: QUICK REFERENCE TABLE

This table is designed to help instructors select case studies that match particular chapters in *Organizational Communication: A Lifespan Approach* by Michael W. Kramer and Ryan S. Bisel (Oxford University Press, 2017). The chart that follows is based upon a combination of the editors' and authors' suggestions. Of course, these are only suggestions. Many of the cases could be used for multiple chapters in the textbook. For example, nearly all of the cases could be used to study organizational culture (Chapter 6). There are leadership (Chapter 8) and power (Chapter 11) implications in many of them. As a result, instructors are encouraged to use them creatively in connection with any chapter that seems appropriate. We believe the richness of the case studies allows for that flexibility.

Case Studies	Textbook Chapters														
	1	2	3	4	5	6	7	8	9	10	11	12	13	14	15
CS 1	X			X											
CS 2		X											X		
CS 3		X													
CS 4		X					X								
CS 5		X	X												
CS 6		X	X											X	
CS 7		X	X												
CS 8			X	X											
CS 9	X		X				X								
CS 10				X	X										
CS 11					X	X									X
CS 12					X		X								
CS 13						X	X								
CS 14					X										X
CS 15							X	X		X					
CS 16								X				X			
CS 17								X	X						
CS 18								X	X						
CS 19										X					X
CS 20				X						X					
CS 21											X		X		
CS 22											X				
CS 23											X	X			
CS 24												X	X		
CS 25							X						X		
CS 26													X	X	
CS 27													X		X

AUTHOR BIOS

Lindsey B. Anderson (PhD, Purdue University) is an assistant professor in the Department of Communication at the University of Maryland. Her research examines the intersections of communication and age in the workplace and has appeared in *Public Relations Review*, *Management Communication Quarterly*, and *Communication Studies*.

David Askay (PhD, UNC Charlotte) is an assistant professor in the Department of Communication Studies at California Polytechnic State University. His research focuses on technological platforms and organizing. His research is published in journals such as *New Media & Society* and *Management Communication Quarterly*.

Darius M. Benton (PhD, Regent University) is an assistant professor of Communication Studies at the University of Houston-Downtown in the areas of Organizational and Religious Communication. His research focuses adolescent social identity formation within organizational contexts and impression management of unethical religious leaders.

Deanna L. Bisel (BBA, Washburn University) is a philanthropist and retired business owner. She has 40 years of work and management experience in the printing and graphics industry. She serves on several executive advisory boards.

Ryan S. Bisel (PhD, University of Kansas) is professor in the Department of Communication at the University of Oklahoma. His research interests focus on leadership communication and behavioral ethics. His research is published in outlets such as *Management Communication Quarterly* and *Human Relations*.

Rebekah Carnes (MA, Kansas State University) is a PhD student in the Department of Sociology, Anthropology, and Social Work and the Peace Corps campus coordinator at Kansas State University. Her research interests include gender, globalization, international development, and environmental sociology.

Kate M. Delmo (PhD, University of South Australia) is a lecturer at the School of Communication, University of Technology Sydney. Her research interests are in the areas of internal communication, organizational communication, and crisis public relations.

Sean M. Eddington (MS, Northwest Missouri State University) is a doctoral candidate in the Brian Lamb School of Communication at Purdue University studying organizational communication. Eddington's research interests exist at the intersections of organizational communication, online organizing, resilience, and gender.

Jeremy P. Fyke (PhD, Purdue University) is an assistant professor in Communication Studies at Belmont University. His research focuses primarily on ethics and leadership development. His work has been published in journals such as the *Journal of Applied Communication Research*, *Human Relations*, and *Journal of Business Ethics*.

Elena Gabor (PhD, Purdue University) is an associate professor in the Department of Communication at Bradley University. Her research focuses on vocational socialization for careers that start in childhood. Her work is published in journals such as *Qualitative Research in Organizations and Management* and *Journal of Ethnographic and Qualitative Research*.

Angela N. Gist-Mackey (PhD, University of Missouri) is an assistant professor in the Department of Communication Studies at the University of Kansas. Her research focuses on social mobility and power in organized contexts. Her research is published in journals such as *Communication Monographs*, *Organization Studies*, and *Communication Education*.

Carrisa S. Hoelscher (PhD, University of Oklahoma) is an assistant professor in the Department of Communication at Missouri State University. Her research examines communication-based tensions in the context of nontraditional or unique groups, organizations, and interorganizational collaborations. She has published research in academic journals such as *Human Relations*, *Management Communication Quarterly*, the *Journal of Applied Communication Research*, and *Small Group Research*.

Anne Kerber (PhD, Ohio University) is an assistant professor in the Department of Communication Studies at Minnesota State University, Mankato. Her research focuses on the intersections of health and organizational communication, and it has appeared in journals such as *Health Communication* and *Management Communication Quarterly*.

Emma E. Kinney (MA, Michigan State University) is pursuing further graduate work in Human Resources Management. She has interests in paternity and maternity leaves, employment interviewing, and leader–member relationships.

Michael W. Kramer (PhD, University of Texas) is professor and chair in the Department of Communication at the University of Oklahoma. His research focuses on the socialization/assimilation process of people joining and leaving organizations, along with leadership and decision making. His work examines both employees and volunteers.

Kathleen J. Krone (PhD, University of Texas at Austin) is professor in the Department of Communication Studies at University of Nebraska-Lincoln. Her research is focused on upward influence, conflict, and emotion processes, and it has been published in *Management Communication Quarterly*, *Journal of International and Intercultural Communication*, and the *Journal of Applied Communication Research*.

Jaesub Lee (PhD, University of Texas at Austin) is professor in the Valenti School of Communication, University of Houston. His research focuses on relationship development and maintenance, leadership, risk, and crisis communication. His research is published in *Human Communication Research*, *Risk Analysis*, and *Management Communication Quarterly*.

Kenneth J. Levine (PhD, Michigan State University) is a faculty member in the Department of Communication at Michigan State University. His research examines vocational anticipatory socialization, leadership, brainstorming, and curiosity. He has published in such outlets as *Communication Monographs* and *American Behavioral Scientist*.

Benjamin D. Luttrull (BA, Ball State University) is a master's student in communication and the Media Relations Specialist at the University of Southern Indiana. His research focuses on the polymediation and digital communities around interactive media.

Cynthia L. McCullough (D.Min., Drew University) is a former college president, church pastor, and counselor. Her research focuses on congregational and pastoral responses to domestic and family violence, counseling, mentoring and coaching, and exploring feminist and nonanthropomorphic images of God for faith exploration and psychospiritual healing.

Lacy G. McNamee (PhD, University of Texas Austin) is an associate professor in Baylor University's Department of Communication. Her research focuses on how members negotiate roles and power in nonprofits and is published in journals such as the *Journal of Applied Communication Research* and *Management Communication Quarterly*.

Andrea L. Meluch (PhD, Kent State University) is an assistant professor of Communication Studies at Indiana University South Bend. Her research interests are at the intersections of organizational and health communication with a focus on social support and stigma. Her work is published in journals such as *Communication Education, Southern Communication Journal*, and *Journal of Communication in Healthcare*.

Vernon D. Miller (PhD, University of Texas at Austin) is a professor in the Department of Communication and Department of Management at Michigan State University. His research focuses on the communicative aspects of the employment interview, organizational entry, performance feedback, role negotiation, and organizational change.

Sophie Moll (BA, University of Oklahoma) is a recent graduate of the Department of Communication at the University of Oklahoma. After graduation, she took a position as a research analyst at Outreach Strategies, LLC in Houston, TX.

Melanie Morgan (PhD, University of Kansas) is an associate dean in Purdue's Graduate School and an associate professor in the Brian Lamb School of Communication. She researches aging in the workplace, and her work has been published in *The Journal of Communication*, *Health Communication*, and *Communication Studies*.

Natalie Nelson-Marsh (PhD, University of Colorado at Boulder) is an assistant professor at the University of Portland. Her research focuses on how organizational members create cultural values and beliefs that influence decision-making processes. Her research is published in journals such as *Management Communication Quarterly* and *New Media & Society* as well as in several book chapters.

Greg Ormes (PhD, Texas A&M University) is an assistant professor at the University of Wisconsin-La Crosse. His research considers the relationships that exist between identity/identification, context, and control within organizations and groups.

Joshua M. Parcha (PhD, North Dakota State University) is an assistant professor of Corporate Communication in the Department of Communication at Penn State Hazleton. His research focuses on corporate social responsibility and corporate advocacy. His published articles appear in journals such as *Management Communication Quarterly*, *Public Relations Review*, and *Communication Research Reports*.

Angie Pastorek (PhD, University of Texas at Austin) is program director for graduate programs in organizational communication at the University of Kansas Edwards Campus. Her research and teaching focus on applied communication best practices for organizational socialization, organizational change, communicating for inclusion, and navigating career transitions.

Nicole A. Ploeger-Lyons (PhD, University of Oklahoma) is an associate professor at the University of Wisconsin-La Crosse. Her research focuses on the intersection of organizational and interpersonal communication, in contexts such as workplace relationships, organizational identification, and organizational ethics.

Jessica A. Pauly (PhD, Purdue University) is an assistant professor for the Department of Communication at Utah Valley University. She is an organizational communication scholar with particular interest in identity, social change, religion, and gender. Jessica has published articles on how women who identify as Catholic and feminist negotiate these two seemingly conflicting identities, as well as faculty perspectives of service learning pedagogy.

Jessica M. Rick (PhD, University of Missouri) is an assistant professor of Communication Studies at the University of Southern Indiana. Her research focuses on identity and stigma within the workplace and work/life issues. She has published in the *Journal of Applied Communication Research*, *Journal of Nonprofit Leadership and Management*, and *Journal of General Education*.

Sarah E. Riforgiate (PhD, Arizona State University) is an assistant professor of communication at University of Wisconsin, Milwaukee. Her research concentrates on communication pertaining to public/paid work and private life. Her work has been published in *Communication Monographs*, *Journal of Family Communication*, and *Management Communication Quarterly*.

Frances L. M. Smith (PhD, University of Missouri) is an associate professor in the Department of Organizational Communication at Murray State University. Her research focuses on communication during times of change like retirement, crisis, and decision making and is published in journals such as *Management Communication Quarterly*.

Chigozirim Utah Sodeke (PhD, University of Nebraska-Lincoln) is an assistant professor in the Department of Communication Studies at Eastern Illinois University. Her work is focused on dialogue across difference and learner-centered pedagogies and has been published in *Departures in Critical Qualitative Research*.

Michael Sollitto (PhD, West Virginia University) is an assistant professor in the Department of Communication & Media at Texas A&M University-Corpus Christi. His research explores organizational assimilation and workplace relationships, and it has appeared in journals such as *International Journal of Business Communication* and *Communication Education*.

Eric D. Waters (PhD, University of Texas-Austin) is an assistant professor of Communication Studies in the Diederich College of Communication at Marquette University. His research examines normative rules and information communication technologies (ICTs) in organizations and stakeholder interactions in developing new ventures and small businesses.

David E. Weber (PhD, University of Denver) is an associate professor in the Department of Communication Studies at University of North Carolina-Wilmington. His research focuses on applied organizational communication, the construction of identity in organizational contexts, and the scholarship of teaching and learning.

Marya Wilson (PhD, Fielding Graduate University) is an assistant professor in the Department of Operations and Management at University of Wisconsin-Stout. Her research focuses on the phenomenological aspects of organizational exit for professional women.

Alaina C. Zanin (PhD, University of Oklahoma) is an assistant professor in the Hugh Downs School of Human Communication at Arizona State University. Her research focuses on issues of power and discourse in unconventional organizational contexts. Her research is published in journals such as *Management Communication Quarterly* and the *Journal of Applied Communication Research*.

TOPICAL INDEX BY CASE NUMBER